Endorsements

"This book is practical, provocative, spiritual and inspiring. As Scott reminds us, being lost is not about *where* you are, but *how* you are—when meaning has disappeared from work, relationships, or life. At this time when so many of us are wandering lost in a world increasingly strange and disturbing, we need Scott's invaluable and wise guidance to lead us home."

Margaret J. Wheatley, author of
Leadership and the New Science and, most recently,
So Far From Home: Lost and Found in Our Brave New World.

"Having felt the deep loneliness of being lost," as Hammond so gracefully describes, I was drawn to the healing metaphor of this book. With each story I felt less alone, comforted by the courage of my fellow human beings. This book is a gift to the soul which longs for meaning, and to, in the end, simply come home.

Amanda Dickson, author of *Wake up to a Happier Life,*
cohost KSL Radio Morning Show.

"When I first read Lessons of the Lost, I realized I was lost due to a major career change; it helped me find my way back home. Lessons of the Lost is a compelling survival guide for today's world. Take it with you wherever you go in life."

James Ayres-Amway Corporation

Lessons of the Lost is for helpers. The stories of those lost - in the wilderness, in relationships, in the workplace - and how they survived are compelling and inspiring by themselves. But the survival strategies Hammond identifies are invaluable to anyone trying to help the "lost" find their way home.

Lou Hampton
Executive Communication Coach
SpeakPersaudeInspire.com

"Scott Hammond does a masterful job of crafting powerful metaphors throughout this book by weaving together elements of wilderness, work, life, hope, love, resilience, communication, and leadership. This book is moving and inspiring, and it has motivated me to be more intentional about the deep impact I want to make in my family, work, and community. It has motivated me to search more diligently for those who are lost within my own circles of influence and provides insights and tools that can be helpful in my teaching, service, consulting, and scholarship."

Susan R. Madsen, author of *On Becoming a Woman Leader* and *Developing Leadership*.

"Scott Hammond is a craftsman who takes life's experiences and molds them into lessons for every soul."

Scott Hawes, News Anchor, KSL Television

Scott Hammond paints a clear picture of the fearful plight of the lost, the faithful flight of the found, and draws compelling parallels between being lost in the wilderness and being lost in life and leadership. As Hammond notes, being lost is a time of high learning, and the valuable lessons learned while lost generate wisdom and grace--indeed, amazing grace: for I was lost, now I'm found. I'm home again (the universal heart's desire).

Ken Shelton, editor, *Leadership Excellence*

"Scott Hammond offers a compelling and accessible look into an extremely important topic that is rarely recognized or talked about in our organizations and society. As a professor, I hope every incoming freshman reads *Lessons of the Lost* and uses its inspiring and meaningful narrative to guide them through the inevitable feelings of being lost and disoriented in a new and challenging environment."

Matthew L. Sanders, author of *Becoming a Learner: Realizing the Opportunity of Education*

Scott captures the reader's attention with true life stories of individuals who were once lost and then found while compelling those who remain lost to continue to read on. He subtly challenges the reader to stop and honestly evaluate their current condition and then offers the lost a path back.

Rev. Dean L. Jackson

"Lessons of the Lost" will fly off the shelves simply because it chronicles amazing real-life dramas about people who have been lost, experienced loss, or found their way home. His pages speak to everyone and anyone who has ever felt "lost" in their lives and reveals the miraculous, the courageous, and the dramatic ways in which people find their way home. Scott Hammond's greatest achievement is that he has written a book....NEVER WRITTEN.

Sonja Eddings Brown-"The Kitchen Cabinet"

I feel that this book is a must read for everyone. If you are not one of the lost in life, you most likely know someone who is and this book will help you understand the concept of being lost as well as give you the tools you need to help those who are lost.

Susan Bulanda-Author of "Faithful Friends"

LESSONS of the LOST

*Finding Hope and Resilience in
Work, Life, and the Wilderness*

Scott C. Hammond, PhD

Lessons of the Lost
Finding Hope and Resilience in Work, Life, and the Wilderness

iUniverse books may be ordered through booksellers or by contacting:

iUniverse
1663 Liberty Drive
Bloomington, IN 47403
www.iuniverse.com
1-800-Authors (1-800-288-4677)

Because of the dynamic nature of the Internet, any web addresses or links contained in this book may have changed since publication and may no longer be valid. The views expressed in this work are solely those of the author and do not necessarily reflect the views of the publisher, and the publisher hereby disclaims any responsibility for them.

Any people depicted in stock imagery provided by Thinkstock are models, and such images are being used for illustrative purposes only.

Certain stock imagery © Thinkstock.

ISBN: 978-1-4759-8871-0 (sc)
ISBN: 978-1-4759-8870-3 (hc)
ISBN: 978-1-4759-8872-7 (e)

Library of Congress Control Number: 2013907957

Printed in the United States of America

iUniverse rev. date: 12/18/2014

Dedicated to my team members at Rocky Mountain
Rescue Dogs, and to all those who search.

Contents

Introduction

The wilderness is a place of the unfamiliar and the unknown. It is material or metaphorical. It is mysterious and predictable. It is the best of classrooms where our deepest learning can occur. But it can also kill us.

We have all been lost in a wilderness. Some have faced survival decisions in community disasters or personal trauma. Some have been lost in work, as they've wandered in careers and professions. Some have been lost in relationships. Others have suffered from crippling addictions or health challenges. Some have returned from military service or a difficult overseas work assignment, suffered the death of a loved one, or been fired from a job. Each of these is a form of being lost. If we are not now lost, then we probably know a spouse, a son, a daughter, or a friend who has wandered so far from his or her path that the home community is out of sight. We hurt, and we hurt for them, wanting to have the person reunited with our common community.

Finding lost people in the wilderness, in the workplace, and in life has taught me that being lost is not a geographic problem. It is not primarily a problem of being in the wrong place. It is a mental and spiritual problem. Lost people may be deprived of the basics of food, water, and shelter, but they are first deprived of meaning.

When you restore meaning, you take the first steps toward hope, and hope is the beacon that leads you home.

There are many books, movies, reality television programs, games, and wilderness training that focus on survival skills. They teach clever ways to adapt to a changing environment by starting a fire with primitive means, building a shelter in the forest, or finding clean water or food in the desert. They may also teach you how to relaunch your career, rebuild your relationships, and overcome destructive behaviors. But "surviving" is what you do when you realize you are lost but don't see your way out yet. It is a holding pattern that may deteriorate over time. People who have been lost and have come home can teach us more than just survival techniques. They can teach us how to go beyond survival and thrive, how to realize when we are lost, how to identify the mental traps that keep us lost, and how to create the mental maps that can lead us out of the woods. They can teach us how to change within to adapt to the change in our environment. They can teach us how to find new meaning and hope that leads us home. Their lessons are in this book.

We often assume that lost people know they are lost, that they want to be found, and that restoring them to a familiar environment will solve the problem. The truth is that many lost people do not know they are lost. Some may not want to be found, and restoring them to a familiar environment will not change their sense that they are lost. Until you deal with the mental and emotional aspects of being lost, you will remain lost.

This book is not about how to start a fire, read a map, or build a shelter. Nor is it about extreme adventures in exotic places that corner people in the middle of nowhere in a place they did not want to be. It is about what happens in the heads and hearts of people who are lost and want to come home. I hope it can help people find their way out of the wilderness and back to the safety of their families and communities.

PART I: LOST

Chapter 1:

Lost

I was lost.

Tumbling in grief.

A little boy, five decades old, who had lost his puppy. After fourteen years of hiking and playing together, in 2008 Sammy just stopped. His back legs were paralyzed by a stroke that damaged his mobility but not his spirit. He could not walk, but he still had the big golden retriever smile that I had come to love. Every time I approached him, his tail flapped in the hope that we were going to the mountains for another hike or cross-country ski. He poured out his unrestrained optimism. He was still full of energy and the hope that birds are forever in the bush to chase, even though he had never, in fourteen years caught one. The birds were there ready to fly and mock him, and he was there, ready to chase.

"It's time," my wife said.

I had been contemplating this moment, and I had prepared myself to rationally make the decision and maturely take him to his last visit to the vet. But there was no rationality in me. I was no longer mature. I wanted to keep my puppy. For three weeks,

I had carried him to his food and to relieve himself. I held him and cleaned him. I made three or four appointments to have him "put down." But I broke them without notice. I could not do it. Finally, one night as I visited him in his outdoor dog run, he was lying on his side. This time he could hardly strain his head to greet me. He tried to roll over. I helped. He smiled, as if to say, "Yes, it is time." The next morning I carried him to the vet and held him as he died. My oldest daughter, Becky, in a role reversal moment, comforted me while I cried.

I am sure my daughter was uncomfortable seeing her father cry. She said all the right things about dogs going to heaven and how they really do amplify our love when they reflect it back to us. She also said, "Dad, when the time is right, we'll get you a new puppy."

Sacrilege, I thought. *I am still in mourning, and you are thinking of a replacement dog?*

When the clouds cleared and a few weeks had passed, I really did not want another dog. Dogs love so unconditionally that when they die you cannot help but feel like you did not give them what they deserved. I felt that about Sammy. This combination of grief and guilt was immobilizing. My youngest son, John, sensed this and said, "Dad, your next dog should not be a pet; it needs to be a working dog." John, who at that stage of his life spent his nights swimming in a sea of stuffed animals that loved him unconditionally, was telling me to get a dog that worked. He and my wife both suggested a service dog. Service dogs, I thought, required a few extra hours of training so that they can reluctantly perform tasks humans don't like to do. Little did I know that it takes, on average, eight hundred hours of training to create a service dog. I also thought service dogs were K-9 slaves, forced to do work demeaning for humans. I did not realize that they love—I mean *love*—to do service.

After an appropriate period of mourning, I began looking for another dog. I checked adoption opportunities and visited the backyards of people who should never have dogs, hoping to be a dog rescuer. In one backyard I met a one-year-old golden retriever puppy that had been so neglected that he had no ability to focus. He just lunged at me, hoping for positive human contact while his owner told me, "It's my girlfriend's dog, and she is never here." Clearly, the dog feared the "boyfriend." As much as I wanted to rescue this retriever, I knew that I could not train the already-programmed problems out of the dog, so I kept looking.

I was convinced that the right dog would find me when I was ready. One day, while the family and I were headed for a weekend at our mountain cabin, we stopped in the small Utah town of Coalville and visited a family with a new litter of golden retrievers. There were eight bundles of golden, furry curiosity tumbling around a backyard. The family's children were eager to show off their young friends, but the parents, including the dog mom seemed tired of managing the chaos of this pack of puppy problems.

I came into the brood with an agenda. I followed John's suggestion and looked for a dog to do search-and-rescue work. I produced several tests designed to see if one of these puppies had the drive, persistence, and loyalty to search. In one simple test I showed a puppy a food treat and then put it under a cup. With the first two puppies, once the treat was out of sight, they lost interest. A more persistent puppy pushed the cup around with his nose for a while until it figured out how to knock the cup over and eat the treat. If the puppy can get to the treat in less than twenty seconds, it is just one indicator that it has the persistence to be a good search dog.

One large male puppy with a darker golden coat watched as we tested a sister and then a smaller brother. They were both good puppies, but they failed the tests. They are probably wonderful pets somewhere today, content to fetch newspapers and bedroom slippers. Then the future working dog watched confidently as I placed the treat under the cup. He immediately swatted the cup and devoured the reward. In less than a second, he solved the problem. He then stood between my son John and the rest of the pack as if to say, "Look no further, I'm the one." John, who took an instant liking to the new family member, named him Dusty.

The next day at the cabin I began search-dog kindergarten, training Dusty with simple runways. I would have John hold him by the collar then I would run 50 to 150 feet, saying his name in a high-pitched voice. When I was behind a tree or a bush, John would let the dog go and he would come and find me, knowing that there was a small piece of meat and some puppy play at the end of the find. Before long, even a puppy learns to follow the scent to the source. It is programmed into their deepest instincts. It is part of the prey drive of a wolf that lingers in their DNA. After a while, I changed roles and let John be found. Then we added the next step—the recall, where the dog needs to come back to the master and tell you he has found someone.

Within a few weeks, I began as a training candidate with Rocky Mountain Rescue Dogs, a nonprofit, volunteer search group with thirty years of experience providing canine search support for hundreds of searches in the intermountain western United States. The group is extremely professional and deeply experienced. Jan Holly assessed Dusty and told me he had what it takes to be a search dog, provided that he received the right training. I had assumed that my new colleagues would help me train my dog how to search. What I did not know was how much my dog would train me and help me recover from my grief, bringing me back from being lost.

Dusty progressed easily through the puppy problems, and soon we could see he was a natural at wilderness or area search, where he would run down every human being in range of his nose, a nose that is about two hundred times more powerful than a human's. But still, the recall alert is essential and sometimes takes several years to train. We also began training to do tracking, using a scent article from the victim to follow the path the victim walked, sometimes over miles, directly to the victim.

My training included first aid; helicopter safety; wilderness survival; GPS, map, and compass navigation; search strategy; dog obedience; crime scene preservation; and lost person behavior.

When I began to study the well-developed psychology of how people behave in the wilderness, I came face-to-face with my own "lost" experience on LaMotte Peak of the High Uintah Mountain Range in Utah, which is detailed in an upcoming chapter. A large database managed by NASAR (National Association for Search and Rescue) has examined the outcome of thousands of searches, developing a probability based set of predictors for lost persons. People who are suicidal are most likely to climb up to higher places. Young children of a certain age are most likely to hide, while older children wander. Right-handed people are more likely to choose the right fork of a trail, while left-handed people are more likely to choose the left. Fishermen, climbers, and hunters all have profiles that predict where they might be.

At the core of this well-developed literature are the stories of how people lost in the wilderness came to be deprived of basic needs, affiliation, identity and meaning. I recognized this behavior, because I have been lost. I realized we have probably all been lost. Not just in the wilderness, but in work and in life. Over time, as I met survivors like Victoria Grover, Rita Cretien and Sue and Ray Baird, whose stories I recount in this book. I realized that embedded in every story of the lost are lessons. The lessons are profound.

For the first year, I attended meetings and training sessions every month, but almost daily I worked with Dusty on obedience and basic area search and tracking. An area search is when a dog is asked to go into a space and find whoever is there. An area search is the most common kind of search problem, because the searchers most often do not know where the subject started getting lost. But most search dogs also need to know how to track. Tracking is used when the searcher knows where the subject was last seen. If the searchers have a scent article that they can present to the dog then the dog, with his magnificent nose, can sort through all the scents and find the track of unique skin rafts (small particles of dead skin) to the subject. Tracking is particularly fun, because the training trails are often marked, so you can see instantly if your dog is doing it right. Most often, they do.

First Callout

It is hard to explain the level of excitement you feel when the pager you have been carrying around for months finally goes off. It tells the world that you have just become an essential part of something important. I wanted my pager to go off while I was teaching a class, in an important meeting, or at the dinner table with family so whomever I was with would recognize my importance. I would make a conspicuous exit and say something like, "My work here is done. I'm needed elsewhere." Instead, it went off when I was in the shower. At first I thought it was a warning from one of the many electronic gadgets in our modern home. But naked and dripping wet, I fumbled around in the pockets of my pants to find the annoying beep of the little electronic box.

I had been carrying around a pager for three months, and aside from a test page, it was beginning to feel like ornamental belt jewelry—one more thing to remember to find before putting my clothes in the laundry. Still, the pager represented something important to me: I was an official SAR "ground pounder." My dog was not certified to search yet, but I was. I could carry water, give support, and learn from my colleagues. After two searches and a test, I would qualify to go out with my dog.

I exited the shower, a bit scared but trying to stay contained. I called Barb, the Rocky Mountain Rescue Dogs dispatcher. Barb is as crusty and kind as they come. She is a former high school gym teacher turned ski resort manager. When sheriffs call Rocky Mountain Rescue Dogs, she drops what she is doing and answers the phone. If the call is in an area where we can help, she triggers the paging system that goes out to about twenty volunteers who call a recorded message to receive their instructions. In my haste, I called the wrong number. Barb kindly reminded me to call the "hotline" and not her, as she needed to keep the line open for updates and communication during an active search. A large percentage of our cases get called back. That is, before we can get to the incident command center, the victim is found and the search is called off. In this case, however, with the search now in its eighth day, it was unlikely that we would be called back.

In my first official callout as a candidate for Rocky Mountain Rescue Dogs in 2009, six of us were asked by the Elko County Sheriff and the Wendover Nevada Police to search for a man who had been missing in the desert for eight days. Within a few minutes, Jan Holly picked me up at my house, and we headed west in her black truck with her well-trained golden retriever, Scout, in the backseat and Celtic rock blaring on the radio. We headed north and then west on the freeway, across the Bonneville Salt Flats to Wendover, Nevada, a casino town just across the border from Utah. About two hours from Salt Lake City, it is a tacky and bright oasis between the salt flats and the desert.

During the drive across the desert, I learned something new about my search-and-rescue mentor. I knew her to be a fiercely independent but loyal mother and wife who volunteered for almost every search. Her years of backpacking, trekking, skiing, and understanding of the K-9 mind made her a perfect candidate for search and rescue. As a volunteer, she had jumped in with both feet, getting National Search and Rescue Association (NASAR) certifications for both herself and her dog. She had mentored others, and me, teaching us basic dog obedience, area search, and tracking. She helped manage the organization and made numerous guest appearances at schools and in the media. This I knew about Jan. But I did not know that she had been lost. I learned that day that Jan is also a recovering alcoholic.

Most of the people I have met while doing search and rescue have been lost. Not in the woods but in the midst of friends, loving family, children, and society. Now twelve years sober, Jan still attends a support group three times a week. "I bottomed out when my kids found me passed out on the kitchen floor," she told me. "They called 911 because they thought I was dead."

As we approached the Utah-Nevada border, Jan got serious about the pending search and began describing her search strategy to me. Jan had been designated Incident Commander (IC), and this was her first time in that role on a real search. Her conversation with me was a self-rehearsal of her own ideas. She wanted to get it right.

When we arrived in Wendover, Nevada, the city police and the Elko County Sheriff ushered us into their conference room in a makeshift collection of city buildings. While this was hardly a one-sheriff town, it was a town where sheriff, police, and highway patrol all knew each other and regularly backed each other up.

Although this search was being conducted by the Wendover City Police, the sheriff and other deputies were helping out. In our briefing, we learned the victim had driven about ten miles to a dusty highpoint in an empty desert. His truck had become stuck in the desert. The sheriff had found the man's truck and searched the area for eight days. The victim was a sixty-four-year-old married man who was an unemployed alcoholic and with a heart condition. On at least three occasions, he'd been in similar situations where he had driven out on one of the many dirt roads in the area, gotten stuck, and walked back to town.

After the briefing, a procession of vehicles headed out to the PLS (point last seen), ten miles from the city in the open desert. From up on a rocky rise at the PLS, you could see one hundred miles across the salt flats to the east and ten miles to the north where the city of Wendover and connecting highways were the only signs that people lived in this part of the world. The victim had driven his truck 2.2 miles off the highway, following a maze of dirt roads created by target shooters, rabbit hunters, and beer drinkers.

Jan had carefully thought out the search strategy and shared it with others. Knowing that by now we were probably looking for a body, we would search based on two assumptions. The first theory was that the victim could see Wendover, misjudged the distance, and tried to walk home. Jan assigned Marie and her bloodhound, Guinness, and her rookie ground pounder (me) to work that part of the problem. The second theory was that the victim had tried to walk back to the highway. She assigned herself and two others from Rocky Mountain Rescue (Kacy and Dee) a quadrant or area between the truck and the highway to search using this theory.

Each dog wore a GPS collar, so we could tell what area they had covered, though in this terrain the dogs are rarely out of sight from their handlers. Kacy and her dog, Uinta, took the quadrant farthest to the south, downwind from the highway, so that the scent of the victim would blow to the dogs and lead them in. That is exactly what happened.

After searching for a little longer than an hour, the incident command center called: "Attention all RMRD units, return to IC (incident command). Ethel/Fred." The first part of this message serves as an indication that the victim has been found. The second word "Ethel/Fred" is an informal code that says the victim is dead.

Uinta, with her handler Kacy, had moved across his search pattern once and then beelined toward the highway, following the scent cone of the victim just beyond the highway. At that location, there was evidence that the victim had arrived at the highway disoriented, crossed the road, and fallen down, dying from exposure on the first night that he was lost. Police confirmed that the victim had also consumed a pint of Vodka on his way to his demise.

When I arrived at the scene, the small-town police and sheriffs were managing the crime scene. The dog handlers were busy with their dogs. I was surprised to see a small Asian woman standing fifty feet from the body and crying. "She's the wife," someone said.

There are two theories about dealing with the victim's family members. The first is to let only the investigating officer have contact. That way, misinformation and false hope will not poison the essential cooperative relationship. That is the more "professional" way. The second is to just be human. Talk to them. Cry with them. Go through it with them.

The second way was thrust upon me, because I was the only person without something to do. The handlers had their dogs ramped up and following the emotions of their handlers. The police had a crime scene until otherwise determined. I walked up to her, and she melted into my side, crying and laughing, chattering away about how well she cared for her husband.

"He drank. He drank all the time," she said. "I was a good wife. I fixed him dinner every night before I go to work. He liked my soup." She told me about his life, his alienation from his family, his arrests, and his drinking. Then, in her somewhat broken English, she told me something I will never forget. "You know," she said. "He was lost a long time before he went missing."

Lost before Missing

No one is lost alone. Everyone who has been called a "victim" brings a social network of human connections into the wilderness. Family and friends, some of them long gone or in dysfunctional relationships, come into the wilderness in some way. Their voices echo in the victim's mind, for better or worse. Strangers also follow you into the wilderness—searchers, therapists, clergy, law enforcement, and bystanders.

Each one of these people who care enough to search for a victim experiences the "lost" incident in a different way. Like the layers of an onion, there are layers of lost that help us understand the lost experience. Each lost experience is unique—for the victim and for the searchers. When lost, you need to know that those who are connected with you are also experiencing your being lost just as you are. Some may see you as isolated, separated, deviated, and even lost before you realize that you are lost. Some victims may go through difficult feelings of depravation or realization before anyone knows they are missing.

Psychologist Karl Weick says most of us go through life as if driving a car using only the rearview mirror. Our ability to make sense of an experience once lived is much greater than our ability for sensemaking in the future. Retrospective sensemaking is that ability to see and understand the incremental stages of being lost that we have gone through in the past. (Weick 2001) In order to shift from understanding what happened to what is happening now, in order to move from understanding history to preventing an undesirable future, we need to move our thinking into the present. We need to see ourselves in real time in each of these layers and act appropriately. Even for someone as strong as Victoria Grover, it is not easy.

My new friend who lost her husband in the Wendover desert was wise to note that her husband was *lost* long before he went *missing*. For him, the first layer of being lost was when he wanted to separate from his family, deviated from rules in his community, and began heavy drinking. When sober, he would begin to drown in his isolation, realize his situation, and try to escape. This deviation continued with minor brushes with the law over the rest of his life, often ending with a night in jail. His escapes, which first seemed like a quest for adventure, led to anxiety and depression as he separated now physically from his support community. Soon, an addiction to alcohol began to limit his choices. He lost hope and self-respect and spiraled into a life as a perpetual victim. In his state of deprivation, a loving woman took him in and cared for him, and at times, he was happy. When he lost his job and gave up looking for a new one, he got in the habit of driving his truck out in the desert and drinking. This time he got stuck and tried to walk toward the highway. I do not know when he realized his state of being lost, but I do know that this time he was not reunited with the few people left in his life.

For this man, and for many others, lost is not a single event. It comes in layers that are placed over the victim, gradually impacting their ability to see, taxing their resilience, and drawing down their reserves.

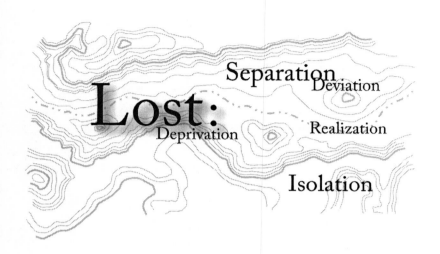

Separation

For searchers, the most important point in any search is called the PLS, or point last seen. In a wilderness search, this is the place searchers are sure that the victim has been. In an ideal search, where others have not contaminated the space, a tracking dog is used to pick up the scent of the victim and follow a track to establish the direction of travel or even find the victim. The PLS is where the lost person has now separated from his affiliations. A person who is lost may be one of the last to be able to identify when he physically separated from his community. The person is often blind to his own situation, especially the severity of it.

It is not surprising that most victims walk past their own PLS never aware that this place will become so significant when they are determined to be lost. It might be their last point of familiarity, but generally, it is the place where the search begins. From this point, searchers speculate how far the victim could or would travel, what path he would take, and why he would take a particular path. The predictive psychology of searching says that different categories of people get lost in different ways. Fishermen stay close to water. Climbers go up. Hunters go across country. My friend and veteran SAR volunteer John Valentine observed that the predicting psychology does not include profiles for extreme sports or high-risk enthusiasts or the despondent. Still, SAR commanders create a theory for the search that includes asking what the victim had in his pack, his level of experience, and a frank discussion with relatives about his mental state and substance abuse.

Several years ago a student of mine, in a reflective paper he wrote, described his first steps into addiction with this paragraph: "I started by not showing up to Sunday dinner. My dad would just rag on me so I stopped going. It seemed like a good thing at the time, but I was cutting my safety net. I started looking for new friends who took me to new places that I just could not handle.... If I were to say when I started, it wasn't when I tried meth; it was when I cut my ties with family."

Place has an important role in the human psyche. It is our common connection with community. The PLS is when we are in our place of safety. Writer Wendell Berry (1972) said, "If you don't know where you are from you don't know who you are." While the boundaries are sometimes unclear, if you step away from where you are from for too long, you begin to lose the sense of being with others that is the anchor we all need.

Separation is the first layer of being lost. Tim Fisher, a search-and-rescue veteran from hundreds of searches in the Pacific Northwest, told me that, "People can generally afford one mistake in the wilderness. They are usually prepared for that. It's the second mistake where things get difficult. The third mistake can be fatal." As we add layers of being lost, we make our second and third mistakes and move closer to what can be fatal.

Isolation

Isolation is another layer of being lost. It means that a lost person is no longer in a social or psychological state where she participates in work community and social events. She is disconnected, whether socially or physically. She is removed from the network of human interaction. This isolation, which may or may not be intentional, cuts the subject off from vital information and creates a sense of "aloneness" that can be devastating. While seen as a defense mechanism against stress, social isolation often causes reality distortion and damages self-esteem. For example, in the next chapter, Victoria Grover, who was lost in the Utah desert, described becoming extremely angry with her son. "I was sure that he just didn't care that I was out in the middle of nowhere with a broken leg," she said. After the incident, she learned that at the time of her anger fit, her son did not even know she was lost. Realizing that she was isolated from reality was as traumatic as realizing she was lost.

Isolation is different from separation because it is social and psychological. Military groups, such as the Navy Seals, work to create exceptionally strong social bonds so that when Seals are separated in combat situations they will not feel isolated from the team. They know that isolation creates "lone wolves" who do not focus on their mission. Similarly, well-run corporations work hard to increase social bonds and communication with employees. Good global companies are particularly careful with employees who have overseas assignments, enhancing communication and funding travel so that they will not feel the trauma of social isolation. While many fictional depictions of searchers show the "rogue" searcher following a "hunch," real searchers avoid isolation. We use radio, GPS spot trackers, satellite phones, and teamwork—lots of teamwork—to learn to communicate and work together.

Deviation

Deviation can be yet another layer of being lost. The Oxford English Dictionary (2003) gives one definition of deviation as "the deflection of a vessel's compass caused by iron in the vessel." This is an apt metaphor for us all. The iron that strengthens our vessel and makes our joints strong can also cause us to deviate. "I don't need my family." "I can handle one drink." "Just a little farther up this trail." "I don't really need a coat." "My pack is too heavy, and I don't really need it." These seem like such inconsequential decisions. But every returning victim can tell you when they made a convenient decision that took him to the next layer of lost.

Deviation is when the victim develops an unrealistic or incomplete view of his situation. Parker Palmer, founder and senior partner of the Center for Courage and Renewal, has written that all knowing is done in a community (Palmer 2004). It stands to reason that when we are separated from community, our knowing suffers. We lose perspective on our own abilities. We act without reliable feedback or input. We fail to consult the map.

For Jason Rasmussen, who became lost while solo hiking in the Boundary Waters Wilderness area, the deviation was not deliberate or conscious. Jason was so comfortable with his abilities that he did not pay attention to the new environment. After being lost for a few days and tired of bushwhacking through thick trees and brush, he became delusional and deviated from rational thought, so decided it would be much easier to hike without his full pack. He abandoned the tent, sleeping bag and food that were keeping him alive. He was lucky that the searchers found these items and eventually found him.

At the point of deviation, people begin to act in ways that seem irrational to the searcher. For example, search dogs are not only trained to find victims; they are also trained to alert searchers to "articles." It is not uncommon for victims to start jettisoning what they think are unneeded articles. In the heat of the day, a victim will drop a coat or jacket because his mental map tells him that when it gets down to freezing overnight he will be snug in bed at home. A victim will jettison a pack, because it is too heavy to carry even though it contains the means to survive for several days. The victim leaves the very things that could save him.

Lost people in work and life jettison career opportunities, relationships, family, religion, and moral values because they are not needed at the moment and appear to be contributing to their loss of meaning. Rather than review, repair, and repent, they cut the line that could lead them home. After a while, deviant behavior stuns the victim into a state of denial or realization. If she denies her situation, she might be able to go on for some time in her false state. If she realizes she is lost, she has taken the first step toward home.

Realization

After he jettisoned his pack, Rasmussen realized his mental state had changed. He realized he had become his own worst enemy when he needed to be his own best friend. Cary Griffith writes, "Suddenly he's claustrophobic, barely able to breathe. He begins to wonder if he will ever find his way out of these woods. Tears start rimming in his eyes. His vision blurs. He can't see anything. He cannot see the bog in front of him, the forest through which he came, even the ground in front of his face." (Griffiths, 2006)

When we realize that we are lost, we begin to see our surroundings as the cause of our predicament. But to avoid this stunning realization, we often deflect the weight off our own shoulders and blame someone else or the environment. We don't want to own up to the choices that led to separation and deviation, so we look to the vast unknown. The woods are to blame—the environment, the economy, globalization, that professor, that boss, that partner who betrayed me, the partner who failed to be perfect. For Jason Rasmussen, the weight was more than he could bear. "The huge body of invisible wilderness weighs on him. He can feel its heaviness on his chest. He can feel his temples pound. He slumps at the edge of the bog and tears spill from his eyes, creasing his haggard face." (Griffiths 2006: 167)

In this emotionally charged state, meaning and reason become illusive. It is only when we can recover meaning that we can begin to be found. "He cannot believe anything. He tries to get a hold of himself, tries to calm his hiccupping desolation, to recover his reason, but there is nothing" (178). Eventually Rasmussen was found, but like Victoria, he still has emotional scars that came from his intense learning experience.

Amy Racina (2005) had a similar point of realization in an autobiographical description of being lost in the Sierra Nevada Mountain Range in northern California. She also faced recovering meaning and reason before she could take the right steps to be saved. During a solo hike in August 2003, Amy fell sixty feet onto a boulder. "In less than a heartbeat," she wrote, "I was betrayed. The friendly landscape turned traitor. The rock gave way. The tree renounced its hold. I hurtled downward. Seconds later, here I am. Lying smashed on the bottom of a ravine" (29).

Racina was critically injured and had fallen into a place where she could not be seen or heard. Too injured to walk or even crawl, over a period of two days she moved herself to a place where she could be rescued using sheer will and persistent courage.

For Racina the point of realization was a point of paralysis. At this moment, people truly realize that they are lost; it comes as such a deep psychological blow that they cannot recover. They become overwhelmed by shame and fear. They lose the will to live. The realization that you are lost, injured, divorced, broke, unemployed, unemployable, sick, bereaved, or radically changed in any way can hit like a tidal wave. It is a gut punch to the emotions and a stab to rational thought. Some just sit down and wait for the end to come. Some deny and keep the realization at bay. But not Amy Racina.

After working though the emotions of guilt and shame, the self-criticism for taking a wrong step, and the idea that she might be being punished for something, she came to a powerful realization. "I want to live," she declared.

> Now, faced with the ultimate question, "How much do you want to live?" I find I do, very much, want to live. There is no doubt whatsoever. Despite my understanding that there are no guarantees, I determined to do whatever I can to make life the probable outcome. I want to live. The sweet swift monument of total assurance becomes a treasure in my memory, because for one glowing second, I experienced absolutely no ambivalence. My decision is made.... I want to live (189).

At the point of realization, we are overwhelmed by equivocality, the sheer number of possible meanings. The mental models, the maps, and the metaphors no longer work. The technology, psychology, and relationships that once guided you now produce confusion. French Pioneer Social Philosopher Emile Durkheim used the term *anomie* to describe what happens to a person when he comes to the realization point and is overwhelmed with equivocality. There is a gap between the social mores and individual circumstances. This mismatch between what is going on in the environment and what is happening in the mind of the individual is a prerequisite to the hopelessness that is the root of suicide, according to Durkheim (1979).

Deprivation

Realization is the point when you have a true understanding of your situation. Deprivation is the point when hope is lost. Not all lost people experience deprivation; many would say it is "touching the void" or at the core of the lost experience. Laura Hillenbrand's book *Unbroken*, which documents the World War II experience of Phil Zamperini, describes his psychological state of deprivation. Zamperini and his friend Louis survived the crash of their B-24 bomber in the Pacific. After forty-two days at sea in a rubber raft, they were captured by the Japanese. In the routinized humiliations of the prison camp, Zamperini experienced greater deprivation than he did living without food and water or shelter on the rubber raft. Louis later recounted his amazing story of survival, admitting that his sense of self was being corrupted by his separation from place and the regular humiliation from guards. He says, "I was literally becoming a lesser human being (183)."

Every lost person I interviewed during my research described a feeling of deep shame that he or she experienced when first were lost. Many of the feelings that lost people experience in this stage of deprivation come because they realize the gap between their current state and the expectations that others have for them. While these emotions can be debilitating, this place of depravation can be an essential milepost for change. You must pass it before there is a felt need to become different. Many of the successful addiction recovery programs will only admit a patient after he has "hit bottom" or "bottomed out."

Earlier in the chapter I described how my colleague and mentor in Rocky Mountain Rescue Dogs, Jan Holly, splits her time between helping find people lost in the wilderness and people lost to addiction. She is a recovering alcoholic who, after many years of sobriety, remains deeply committed to helping others come home.

Jan has also helped mentor alcoholics in a twelve-step process to find the path to sobriety. As we work our dogs, she often receives a call from someone she is guiding to sobriety. I have also heard just her side of the conversation as she has turned a person down who was asking for a mentor.

I asked Jan about how she selects those whom she will mentor and those she will not. "It's simple," she says. "If they have bottomed out, then they are ready for the difficult path to sobriety. If they have not, then everyone's best effort can't keep them from drinking again."

I have attended some of the meetings to help me understand how they help people lost to addiction. As people rise and give the familiar, "Hi, my name is Joe, and I'm an alcoholic," you realize that their stories almost always include a point of deprivation when, as one person said, "everything went black."

For Jan the point of deprivation came when she blacked out, waking up only to see her two small children watching as their mother was wheeled into an ambulance. Jan spent three days in the hospital and said, "I realized how much I loved my little boys and their father. I never wanted them to go through that again."

Jan is clear that bottoming out is different for everyone, but without it, there is insufficient motivation to change. So Jan is now a searcher. With Scout, she searches for lost people in the wilderness. With AA, she helps people along the way to sobriety. Every lost person needs to know that beyond family and friends there are searchers like Jan who will help him find his way home.

Deprivation can be positive or negative. It can lead some to the point of giving up, while others find a new kind of strength that helps them survive long enough to be rescued and to thrive. For the survivor, deprivation induces a proactive humility that helps her acknowledge her own vulnerabilities to the wilderness or to substance. It fuels the strength needed to move into more positive behaviors—wayfinding behaviors.

Hope

Hope is the subject of the final section of this book, but it is important to note at this point that people who are really lost and who come home are forever changed when hope is regenerated from the deep fear of being lost. A true lost experience leaves a deep mark on the soul. Lost stories are personal, difficult, transforming, and sacred. My story of being lost is the subject of the next chapter. In each of the next chapters, people have shared their sacred stories about being lost. Each chapter develops one of the "lessons of the lost." Each chapter also contains a sacred story or stories of people who were saved by persistence, change, and hope. I am grateful to be trusted by each to give words and voice to their narratives.

For Jan, telling the story of her alcoholism after twelve years of sobriety means revisiting the darkest period of her life, but it also helps her reaffirm a commitment to stay sober. For Amy Racina, the solo Sierra hiker whose fall led her to the realization of how much she wanted to live, reunification taught her life-changing lessons:

> I have learned to hold on tightly to what I've got, to cherish it and appreciate it and love it, because in the flash of a footprint, it could all be gone. I am not as quick to attach permanence to anything that I hold dear, but I am more inclined to savor the many joys, to look about me and treasure the golden moments and all the blessings that I find. I have learned that even when I go solo, I am not alone.

"Mental Maps and Mental Traps"
Use the QR code on your smart phone to watch an eight-
minute video on lost person behavior produced by the author.
(Also available at lessonsofthelost.com)

Chapter 2:

Overdressed

Victoria Grover wore a dress when she hiked. She wore pants underneath, but it was the dress people saw. On the trail she endured the snickers of teenagers and the bold questions of a youngster asking in a loud voice, "Why is that woman wearing a dress?" But it was her signature wear. The jumper was the informal uniform of the clinic where Victoria had worked as a physician's assistant for twenty-six years. It made her look professional and well dressed, yet it allowed for the movement her five foot two frame needed while examining patients. It brought the perfect balance of form and function.

On this bluebird day, in April 2012, 2,500 hundred miles from her home in Maine, wearing a dress on a desert plateau in Utah would save her life.

Nowhere

With wedding bells still ringing in her head, she awoke to silence. It was the silence of a small town, not even a town, on the edge of a remote stretch of nowhere—one of those rare places in America where you can see no lights at night except the stars, a single streetlamp, and a Pepsi machine at the two-pump gas station across the street. She had come to the nowhere of southern Utah to escape the somewhere of her little Maine town. For Victoria, the two most beautiful and different places in the world are Maine and southern Utah.

At her Maine home, the health care for her small community rests on her shoulders. At fifty-eight years of age, she had a history of hard work and had earned herself a position as the town's medical provider, a leader in her church, a mother, and a wife. The wedding was her son's—her special son, her youngest son. It had been a wonderful wedding, but the stress of the clinic, the difficulties of the business, the travel, and the busy time with family made her hungry for something she had tasted years before.

Forty years ago, young Victoria had come to the nowhere of the Escalante to find herself. She had enrolled in a university-sponsored, six-week wilderness survival course. It was harder than boot camp, and she had to pay tuition for the privilege of the experience. So why do it? In the early 1970s, the promises of the "new generation" of the sixties were already unraveling. The Vietnam War was ending, and her adult life was just beginning. For Victoria, life was clear as mud. Six weeks in the desert wilderness was sure to bring her closer to what she wanted to be—closer to clarity.

The first day of wilderness survival began with a sixteen-mile hike through a land that seemed like another planet. The Escalante in southern Utah is a remote red rock desert carved by wind and water. Shade trees grow only near water, and water in the Escalante is hard to find. Sand, rock, sage, and dirt dominate the landscape of the desert. Yet, in this arid land, one can learn to find all the resources needed to survive and even thrive. The Pueblo, the Hopi, the Navajo, and the Fremont had all found ways to make the desert their home. The young Victoria was sure she would too.

On day one Victoria was given a canteen, a map, and a compass and told where to go. For a while she followed the others, but her short legs could not keep up. Already in the every-man-for-himself mode, the group moved on, leaving Victoria to face the empty desert alone. Terrified, hopeful, proud, and wondering, she moved toward her distinction and, hopefully, her clarity. She was already changing, though her consciousness was just focused on the next step, the right direction, and the conservation of precious water. The wilderness was already teaching. The first lesson was about the economy of movement. The second was the simplicity of real wealth. The desert was beginning to show her clarity of purpose and a path that she would carry with her for the rest of her life.

With blisters blazing and tongue withered like a raisin, she stumbled into camp, the last of the weary hikers to complete the near death march. The one-quart of warm water issued at the beginning of the hike was long gone. The green and brackish liquid relief that was offered quenched every ounce of her driving thirst. A baked, though mostly burnt, potato cooked directly on the fire was presented. Forty years later, she still thinks of it as one of the best meals she had ever had. The wool blanket on the hard ground felt like a feather bed in a five-star hotel. It was dark, and the desert heat was turning to cold. In the next two hours the air temperature would drop 50 degrees. But Victoria slept.

The stabbing morning light brought a harsh reality of aching muscles and complete remoteness. From their first camp, the survivalists could not see any sign that other humans graced the planet. With the rising of the sun came the heat, the sweat, and the dust that would become so familiar. At some points for the next few days, she would slip into the old Victoria, the one left at the edge of the wilderness who just wanted to go home. But each day the new Victoria became stronger, smarter, and more comfortable in this environment. She learned where to find water, what to eat, and how to navigate with and without a map. At night she would peer into the universe and see her own soul wandering, lost, looking for a place. At first this image scared her, but after a while she became comfortable with her new homelessness.

The old Victoria would not think about the future, only the present—the next drink, the next meal, the shelter needed for the night. Was she traveling the right direction? Was she going to arrive at the destination before dark? Then slowly, as the new Victoria grew, her time horizon changed, and she began thinking in terms of days, weeks, and even years. After five weeks of hardship and learning, she would "solo." She was given her own patch of desert wilderness where she would remain alone for five days. For some in this group the solo seemed like an insurmountable challenge. But Victoria saw it as an opportunity. "I had been looking to find myself in a future," she told me. "This would be the time."

Under the desert stars, where quiet was interrupted only by the sound of the wind and an occasional bird, Victoria laid out her life's plan. Her journal, written in pencil, and with red dirt still embedded in the cover, documented her social and spiritual commitments, her goals, and her clarity. The journal was the vessel that she would use to carry clarity out of the desert and back to a world where noise and ambition obscured.

Forty years later, the clarity was spent. The new Victoria had become old.

So on this bluebird day in April 2012, after the wedding of her youngest son in Provo, Utah, her family returned to Maine, and she headed to the desert to recapture clarity. Still on a tight schedule and surrounded by adult responsibility, she had only one week before the strings of the clinic, the needs of the community, and the opportunity to serve in her church would draw her back. One week to find the new Victoria again.

She did not know that this wilderness experience would be even more profound than the first.

Survival 2.0

Victoria left the wedding, her husband, and her family and headed south. She followed the high-traffic I-15 to where it merged with I-70. Much of the traffic at this point was headed to lose themselves in the bright lights of Las Vegas. She hoped to find herself in the quiet of the Escalante. In Cedar City she turned east, where things began to look familiar. Surely those same stars, that same clear sky, and those red rocks and cliffs would help her see her future again.

Forty years of day hikes and twenty-six years in a clinic in Maine had tempered her risk taking. This time her agenda was less ambitious. There would be no sixteen-mile solo treks without a trail, no building her own shelter, and no sleeping in a wool blanket on the hard ground. She would stay in a small hotel near the Grande Staircase Escalante National Monument and go on day hikes. She hoped the solo time in the room and on the trail would take her to clarity and give her another adventure that would last another forty years.

In the backseat of her car was a simple backpack. Victoria always went simple—a lingering lesson from wilderness survival forty years earlier. In her pack were old friends: a two-dollar, never-opened poncho; matches; a canteen; a few first aid items; snack foods; a flashlight; and a map and compass. That was all she needed. That fancy GPS equipment, she would argue, just kept hikers in the technological world. She said, "Besides, what do you do when your GPS runs out of batteries?"

After Cedar City, the traffic thinned. It was a weekday, and there were just a few tourists making their way to Bryce National

Park or Cedar Breaks. It was mostly local traffic now along the winding highway. Farther east—one hour, then two—there was almost no traffic as she approached Boulder and turned toward the Sweetwater Valley. Whoever named places in this country had a real sense of humor. There was nothing sweet about the trickle of water in this valley.

The motel's small parking lot was a quarter full of rental cars, mostly rented by international tourists hoping to notch a visit to a place none of their friends had ever been. Led by either a German tourist magazine or a French version of *National Geographic*, tourists would come to the Escalante, drive around, take a few pictures, and then drive four hours to Las Vegas to spend money on forgettable and mind-numbing experiences. But the stop in the red rock desert would give them a few great photographs and a unique dinner conversation story with no real adventure to attach to it. This place was too empty to keep those used to the crowded spaces of cities for long.

By now Victoria was brimming with anticipation. On her first day she would hike to Salt Creek. In three miles she knew she could leave this patch of humanity behind and be in full wilderness emersion. Tonight she would settle into this clean and new hotel room that would be her monastic living for the next five days—at least that was the plan. Before going to bed, she put her backpack and boots by the front door and hung her jumper over the chair. It would be her only night she spent in that bed.

Vespers

Some people pray on their knees in the dark. They seek God in a church, cathedral, mosque, or temple. But in another kind of devotion, people walking uprightly face the created world, their eyes full of awe. Pretending to stand face-to-face with God, they pour out their appreciative hearts. Victoria knew how to pray both ways. The first kind of prayer she did at home and in church. The second she did on the trail.

She awoke early on the first day. Her body was still two hours earlier, on Eastern Time. Unable to stay in bed, she put on pants and a T-shirt, pulled over her jumper, laced up her boots, grabbed her pack and hiking pole, and walked out of the motel room. Before she got into her car, she filled up the water bottle. Always responsible and knowing she would be alone on the trail, Victoria checked with the motel clerk and asked him to watch for her return. I said, "If I am not back by 9:30 p.m., call for help." The young man agreed, and Victoria adopted the assumption that if she got get lost, they would start looking for her that night.

It was just a short drive to the Coleman Trailhead, but it was still not easy to find. Trailheads in or near the Grand Staircase National Monument are not well marked. While the Clinton administration designated the monument to protect the land ("Protected from what?" ask the locals), Congress has never adequately funded the expansion of the National Park Service (NPS) and National Forest Service (NFS). Good stewards that they are, the NPS and NFS budgets are spent on the high-impact, high-traffic parks like Yellowstone, Zion's, and the Grand Canyon. There would be no park ranger programs on this trail and no lazy-day hikers. This trail was for the serious hiker with a purpose, like Victoria.

The trailhead was just a dusty parking lot with a bulletin board and a few a sun-bleached signs. Did anyone every really read the signs? Victoria was from a generation that did. In the early days, when Victoria was a Girl Scout, the Forest Service posted signs at trailheads that read: "What to do when lost in the woods." This was a time just a half century ago when GPS, cell phones, and helicopter rescue were not even yet in our modern imaginations.

The flyer posted at trailheads around the west began, "Merely being out of sight of others in a strange forest gives many a man the creeps—a natural feeling, but a dangerous one. Never yield to it." It goes on to say, "Loss of mental control is more serious than lack of food, water, or clothing or the possible proximity of wild animals."

Victoria came from a generation when these kinds of words were still spoken around campfires. Forest Service brochures say prophetically, "Keep the old brain in commission and chances are you will come out of the woods on your own two feet."

By the time the sun crept over the red rock horizon, Victoria was on her own two feet and headed down the trail. It had been cold the night before, getting down into the high thirties, but it would be a warm day. At seven thirty that morning, it was already 65 degrees, and it would hit 80 before noon. By then, Victoria hoped to be at Salt Creek with her feet dangling in the cool water. By five o'clock that evening, she planned to be back at the hotel in the bathtub washing the red sand from her dusty feet. It was only six miles, round-trip. In Maine, she would hike after work twice a week. Her favorite route was a four-and-a half-mile loop. She could still do could do it in one hour and forty-five minutes. This would be a bit longer, but she felt up to the task.

So Victoria headed up the trail. It was flat at first, through the cow pastures and broken fences, to a gradual rise to a beautiful meadow. She was already two miles in and making good time. At two and a half miles, she stood overlooking Salt Creek. It was worthy of pause and gaze. She drank in the soul-cleansing view. The Sweetwater Valley behind her was ranch country. The red rock valley in front of her was the nowhere she had come to experience. It was vast and open, with escarpments of red rock the size of railcars stretching north to south. The trail was steep down now, down to the point where three small streams converged. As she followed the trail down, the temperature cooled. The vegetation thickened. She felt the effects of the water before she saw it.

This being a desert, the water was disappointing. Three streams coming together still only made a small stream that barely got her feet wet. It was the spring of a dry year, and by June this would not be a stream at all. But for now there was running water, shade, and cool.

It had taken Victoria a little longer than an hour to travel the first three miles. A return trip, even after a wade in the stream, would mean she would be back in the hotel room by noon. It had hardly been an adventure yet, and there was nothing to do in the hotel room. She decided she would go another mile along what looked like a trail. Explore. Then maybe some bushwhacking up to the red rocks she had seen from above. It would take her another hour, maybe two. From there she would be able to see clearly, across the valley, back to where she had come from, back to Salt Creek, to the plateau, to the Sweetwater Valley, the motel, maybe back to Maine.

She was no longer on an official trail, but there was a pathway. It was not on the map, but it was on the ground. It paralleled the stream for a while and then edged up the north side of the valley. If she followed it too far, she would be in the National Park, but staying to the northwest, she remained in the National Forest. National Forest land in the West comes with grazing rights that, in some cases, have been assigned to family ranches for generations. Victoria was on a cow trail, or a cowboy trail, with all the markings and droppings one would expect. Along the way were cowboy campsites, fire pits, and rusty cans—just too many signs of civilization. Still feeling great, and not ready to turn back, she turned right and headed up to the red rocks in hopes of seeing another cleansing view.

It did not take long for Victoria to start gaining altitude. There was no trail now, and the dust and dirt became rocky. Once she reached the small plateau, she was on pavement. Not man-made pavement, but sandstone pavement where she left no tracks and had great traction. It was easy to walk on, easy to go up. And so she did. Up to the red rock and into the maze of the escarpments.

She stopped, ate, drank, and continued. Seeing the whole valley now, she was higher than her first plateau, higher than she had been at any point when she entered the red rock forest with boulders the size of train cars. The terrain was familiar. She remembered her wilderness solo trip forty years earlier in a setting like this.

At this point, Victoria was surprised at how far she had come, how good she felt, and how beautiful her surroundings were. She was sure that she was the only one in the valley. She was the only one for miles. Her thoughts stretched back to the wedding, her son, and her new daughter-in-law and then to Maine, her husband, her medical practice, and her patients, whom she loved. What a blessing to give health care to generations—to treat a community, not just a group of people. Clarity was coming. It was just around the corner, maybe around the next boulder.

As she hiked, she thought about a recent patient whom she had cared for as long as she had served the little town of Wade. Months before, when Victoria had delivered the news, the worst kind of news, she had promised that she would not let her die in pain. Then a few weeks ago, her beloved patient in her last days of life could no longer get the pain medication she needed. It was part of the national drug shortage, and this patient was desperately in need of strong narcotics to dull the worst kind of cancer pain. Victoria called in every favor from every pharmacy within 250 miles to get what was needed. It was a privilege to serve her, to be her caregiver, to be there in her last precious moments of life.

As the shadows of the late afternoon stretched behind her, a slow, creeping gratitude overwhelmed her. She stood in the shade and began her meditation—her face-to-face prayer that began with an expression of gratitude.

Later Than She Thought

Time had accelerated as clarity seeped into Victoria's mind. It was late afternoon, and she could see it was time to head home. She headed south and down but found herself in a rock maze. Backing out, she tried another way—and another. The sun was on the horizon now. The shadows were deeper. The light was fading fast. She had expected longer days, but it was still spring in southern Utah. But there was no panic, just the confidence that comes with the clarity she had achieved that day. The Girl Scout lessons found on the old Forest Service bulletin were embedded in her mind, just like the diagnostic process she used to determine if a patient had a common cold or pneumonia. She ran through the list in her head:

"Stop, sit down, and try to figure out where you are. Use your head, not your legs."

She thought about spending the night on the mountain. It would create some embarrassment when she returned to the motel or faced a park ranger sent down the trail to look for her, but the thought did not create panic or even concern.

"If caught by night or a storm, stop at once and make camp in a sheltered spot. Build a fire in a safe place."

She had been in a similar situation before. As a twenty-year-old Girl Scout leader on a two-week canoe trip in a Canadian Provincial Park, she had held the group on shore for a day-and-a-half because of high winds. The guides and the girls all wanted to face the winds and the waves, but she had made the tough call. Arriving a day late to waiting parents, they were applauded by leaders and loved ones for being conservative, responsible, and safe. They were also the only group to return without the loss of equipment. Now Victoria reaffirmed to herself that she was not afraid to make the tough decision.

She found a rock heated by the sun. In the sparse vegetation of the desert, it took the last light of the day to find enough firewood for the night. She lit a fire with a single match, conserving the rest for another time. Sitting in the soft sand, in the shelter of a boulder, and facing the way home, she made a plan for the early morning exit. She would head back to the stream and the trail as soon as possible. The searchers would come quickly, she thought, and she would have to apologize for being late. This was the safe thing—the prudent thing—to do. Like the parents by the lake years ago, they would understand.

"Don't yell, don't run, don't worry, and above all, don't quit."

She would not quit. She had no intention of quitting. Quitting was not an option; it never had been. In the morning, early, she would be at the stream. She would refill her now nearly empty water bottle and make her way back to the trail.

"The man who keeps his head has the best chance to come through safely."

This advice applied to women too. She was good at keeping her head. This night would just be another solo. It was another chance to cleanse the soul. No worries. Really. No worries. If she never said anything, her family would not even know she spent a solo night out in the desert.

While she did not sleep particularly well huddled near the fire, this would be her best night of sleep for some time. Snacks filled her stomach. Water quenched her lips. Soft sand was her mattress. A poncho was her blanket. The jumper she always wore while she hiked kept her warm. The shadows and the firelight played off the tall red rocks, and the dancing light brought peace to her soul. The quarter moon was rising. Victoria realized this was the adventure she craved.

The "Little" Drop

There was one time just before dawn, just before the unseen birds began their morning chorus, when Victoria slept deeply—perhaps for an hour, maybe two. It was the light that woke her. Facing the rising sun, the first pink rays stretched over the horizon and brought instant warmth. The fire was just smoldering, and Victoria was sitting close, very close. Her poncho kept the light breeze off.

Now it was time to get off the rocks and into the valley. She spent almost thirty minutes putting the fire out. She did not want to start a wildfire not in this dry and sacred space with red rock cathedral spires. Because there was no water, she poured sand on the ashes and then stirred until the smoke was gone—completely gone.

The water was gone too. She was glad for the dry mouth, because it distracted her from wanting to brush her teeth. She had a few pieces of trail mix and a banana. It was a fine breakfast.

She scanned the horizon and set her sights on getting back to the stream, planning her descent to Salt Creek. She studied the map, looking for the maximum space between lines to indicate the gentlest slope. It looked like the best way would be a more direct route, going north above the confluence of the three streams and then tracking back along the streambed.

Keeping the valley on her right, she moved north across the face of the plateau. At first, she was confident that she could get down at almost any point. Too many steep ledges blocked one attempted descent. She did not want to get stranded where she could not go up or down. So she moved north, past the point where the streams came together. The plateau was less familiar now. It was less red and more neutral. The sun was up. It was past seven, perhaps later, and she needed to get to the trail. She needed to meet the searchers and apologize. She had told the man at the motel to that she would be back at nine thirty. She was now at least eleven hours late. Surely searchers would be preparing to comb the valley. Her urgency was to find them and tell them she was okay. Heaven forbid that they had called her husband and worried the family. Heaven forbid.

The gradual slope led to a ruffled edge where a breaking set of rocks marked a downward passage. It was a steep but still a good place to go down. In the steep parts, Victoria would use her walking stick as a third leg to descend. Below she could see the creek—or *a* creek. It was not as big as the three creeks merged into one, but if she could get to it, she could follow it down to the convergence, to the trail, to the searchers. In her mind, she could see the searchers waiting at the creek, knowing that she would be there soon. She assumed they were already searching for her. But she was wrong—very wrong.

It was steep going down. She would never have gone up this way. Carefully, she descended. Now she was just a hundred, perhaps a hundred and twenty, yards from the stream. She could feel the cool, local climate as she descended into a different ecosystem. She looked forward to a drink of the cool and untreated water. Sure, she would take in some unfamiliar organisms, some strange germs spread by cows wading upstream. She decided a potential stomachache was better than dehydration. But soon her muscles ached, her tongue was dry, and she had a slight headache. She was beginning to feel the first effects of dehydration. But the water was only three hundred feet away. Below her there was a short drop down. Maybe it was a four-foot drop, but she could turn around and slide and drop. That way she would only drop twelve to eighteen inches, then through the tamarack, and to the cool water. It was going to be easy.

It would be twelve hours before she reached the water.

The Hole

Victoria's next move changed everything. She turned around and rolled along the rock, sliding, gripping, and falling. For most people this would not be a drop, but Victoria was short. As gravity took over, Victoria thought this was no longer a controlled fall. As her feet met the sand, there was a snapping sound and then pain—sharp, driving pain. She knew immediately that she had broken her leg. She could see it was the tibia and the fibula. Her foot was out of position as if it were connected to the leg by gelatin. Fighting to change her demeanor from victim to medical professional, she examined the situation. Her bones were just below the surface of the skin. It was almost a compound fracture, with her bone visible just below the surface. She had a walking stick and a few scraps of cloth to make a splint. She had nothing but Tylenol to dull the pain, but it was grossly inadequate for her level of pain.

To make matters worse—and she wondered how they could be worse—she was in a hole created by a dried up waterfall. She couldn't go up, and she could get to the water. If searchers came along the stream, they would not see her. There was a twelve-foot angled rock that now looked more like a cliff between her and the water. Now matters were worse, because she was dehydrating fast in the heat. She needed water or she would die, but moving put her at risk of turning her break into a compound fracture where bleeding to death was a real possibility.

Sitting in the dirt at the bottom of the hole, she began to reassure herself. "By now the searchers are near, probably only a few hundred yards away," she told herself. But in the hole, behind the rocks, they would not see her. *Noise*, she thought. *Loud noise*. She yelled but found her voice did not carry and would not last long. Then she lined up an impromptu set of instruments and began banging in threes. In Girl Scouts, calls for help always came in threes. First she hit rocks together, then her water bottle—always in threes. For the next ten hours she would play her instruments and call for searchers who never heard her, never came, were never there.

The sun was creating deeper shadows now. There were only two or three hours of daylight remaining. With splint in place, she made the decision that she would deal with her most immediate need. She made the tough decision—the kind she was used to making for others. She would go to the water. Despite the pain, despite the possibilities of rescue, without water she would soon be too weak to do anything. Fighting off the effects of shock, she prayed—the face-to-face kind of prayer. Victoria knew she did not have the upper-body strength to get out of the hole. She imagined herself climbing with one leg and two arms facing the rock, holding the rock. If she let go, if she fell, her broken bone would push through her skin, and there would be blood everywhere.

Everywhere. She could not do that, she told God. Together, they would have to find another way.

She prayed with urgency. She had asked God many times in her life to "be lifted up"—lifted up spiritually. This time she wanted to be lifted up literally—up and over the rocks. It was then that she saw the way out of the hole. Go backward. Sit on a ledge. Push yourself up with your good leg. Balance with your weak arms and then sit again, bad leg dangling in raging pain. She planned and studied her ascent, carefully choreographing every move. The first stage worked perfectly. Her small frame made it possible to sit in place most cannot. Up again, with pain following. The splint held, and she fought the instinct to use the bad leg anyway. Up again—now eighteen inches, now two feet from the floor. She was blind to what was behind her, so she felt with her arms, rested, then launched with her good leg and planted with her bum.

With two good legs and two strong arms, this would have taken no more than thirty seconds. It took Victoria fifteen minutes, maybe more. The sun was now over the cliffs. The temperatures were already dropping. With her last heave, she found solid rock. There was no more fear of sliding back into the hidden waterless pit. She was out of the hole and could see a larger world. On the way up she had felt her broken bones grating against each other. Now she could not go down backward, so she turned forward, lifted her broken leg, and scooted an inch or two forward. She repeated the move a thousand times to go about fifty feet to level ground. Her prayer had been answered in a way she had not imagined.

The heat and exertion, the shock and the dehydration had taken their toll, but she had conquered her Everest. Now she had perhaps a hundred yards to cover to get to the water. Knowing the peril of her situation, Victoria began to think about her environment. She was now near the life-giving water, but she was also in the shade where the cool could become cruel cold in a matter of hours. The night before, the fire had warmed her, but the morning still had an edge. In this cool canyon, she expected temperatures to get into the low forties overnight, and next to the stream there would be a breeze that would make it feel even colder. Once she had water, she would need warmth, but without mobility, she could not gather wood.

So as she began the long crawl to the water, over dust and downed trees, she collected every lose stick and piece of grass that she came across. Dragging her poncho behind her, she placed anything that would burn on the plastic surface. By the time she reached the water, the sun was cheating its way out of the canyon. She put her face in the mini torrent, briefly enjoying the cool on her face. Victoria then filled the water bottle, drank, and filled it again. It was the familiar taste of alkali in the water—familiar from forty years earlier when she had lived on water from a stream like that. *Taste and memory*, she thought. *Taste and memory.*

The temperatures were dropping with the fading of the sunlight. The sand around the stream was cold and wet—not the place she wanted to stay at night. Farther from the stream, the sand was still warm from the sun. So she performed the backward crawl again, ten, maybe fifteen feet to a place where she could see her little valley and wait for rescue. "I thought they would be here by now," she told herself.

Before she left the side of the stream, she remembered a scene from her favorite Japanese samurai movie. In this film the hero throws white magnolias into a stream to send a signal downstream to his companions. Victoria took out her journal and tore out a page, cutting it into twelve pieces and writing on each one: "Victoria Grover, upstream, broken leg." Then at sixty-second intervals, she threw the notes into the stream, hoping the rescuers would find them. Proud of her cleverness, she began to crawl back to the warm, dry sand and away from the water. But rescuers never saw the notes; they never came close to the stream, for that matter.

Her next concern was fire. This would be no ordinary fire. She would use an old Native American "trick" and make an ash bed to sleep on. She built the fire long and burnt it hot; when the little pieces were exhausted and the big pieces were smoldering, she placed them in a small trench that she had dug in the sand. Covering the coals with sand, she rolled onto the warming sand and tried to sleep. But even though the sand would keep her lower body warm for the next six or seven hours, sleep was hard to come by.

The Search for Reality

Exhausted and in shock, cold and feeling the pain of grating bones, the battle for survival moved from the environment to her mind. Her body was moving now limited energy to the parts that needed the most. As the darkness enveloped her, she began to hear voices. At first she thought it was the stream, but then she "heard" them—definitely voices, recognizable voices. It was Ben—her son, Ben. Oh, she knew he would come. "We found you, Mom!" he said. There were other voices too. Rescuers—park rangers talking about her but not listening.

"Over here!" she would respond. But then nothing. No one in the nowhere. More voices. Were they making a rescue rig stringing ropes? She heard idol conversation. "Over here! I need a blanket! Come on! You're ignoring me! I would never treat one of my patients that way!" Her voice echoed off the rocks. Then, in the dark, through the trees, she saw a road—yes, a road—where she imagined park rangers were driving rescue vehicles. Yes, coming for her. *It's about time*, she thought. *They are coming for me. I can see them.*

But also in her mind was another voice—a rational voice telling her that what she was seeing was not real. It was telling her that the hallucinations were a result of the chemical imbalance in her body created by pain, muscles breaking down, and dehydration. The rational part of her said, "Drink. Drink and stay real." So she drank, a water bottle every two or three hours, charting her fluid intake as if she were one of her own patients.

The fluid intake created another problem. She could not easily get up and relieve herself in the bushes. So five feet from her little camp she dug another trench—her cat litter box, she called it—to relieve herself in the sand. At needed intervals, she would leave her patch of sand warmed by the coals of her buried fire and scoot to the trench. As she pulled off the layers and relieved herself, she could feel the desert night cold rob the heat from her body.

As the light of morning came, she was still looking for the anchor of reality in her head. She wanted the voices to be real; she wanted Ben to be near and trying to rescue her, but she could see that there were no roads and no rangers. No one had come to her. It was time for a Tylenol from her little pack. She took the pills to dull the pain but hardly felt any effect at all.

The Morning Light

What did have an effect was the morning sun. Just before eight o'clock, the sunlight poured into her little camp, erasing the cold and hallucinations in minutes. Now the world was clear again. The sky was blue, the rocks were red, and the real searchers would come. They would come. She hoped Ben would be with them—Ben, her Boy Scout, her son.

With the biting cold gone and boredom just inches away, she began thinking about what would happen when rescuers would finally come. Would they be angry? Scolding? Respectful? Could they care for her badly mangled leg? It was in these thoughts that she drifted off to sleeping the warm sun—real sleep for the first time in twenty-four hours. Sleep was the only escape from her persistent pain. But worse than the pain was the waiting.

Sometime in the afternoon she woke to the sound of a bird. As her eyes adjusted to the bright light, she saw a large vulture hovering in the trees high above her. Wow, something interesting to see. A creature had come to break the boredom. Interesting. She drifted off in midthought and awoke seconds or minutes or an hour later to the sound of a second bird. Cute. Yes, cute. Vultures seemed so interested, but she planned to disappoint them. She drifted off again. Then she heard more bird sounds and spotted a bird that was getting close—very close.

Enough, she thought. *I'm not dead yet!* Victoria yelled and took her poncho out and waved it. All three birds got the message and left for the open sky, but then Victoria realized that she had just scared away an obvious sign for rescuers. Rescuers often look for birds to lead them to injured people. "Back," she called. "Come back!" But they did not come back, and now the shadows were deepening. She was about to face her third night alone in the Escalante.

Having burnt all the fuel within reach, this would be her first night without a fire. All the heat needed to come from her own body. She had hiked without a jacket, in two T-shirts, pants, and underwear. But the jumper—the signature dress—was the fourth layer. Like pioneer women who wore dresses in the woods, she was grateful for the style, the uniqueness, and the extra layer. Even though she was cold, the extra layer made a critical difference.

She also had the poncho. It was just a two-dollar poncho, barely big enough to give her cover. She would seal up the arms and the head and pull the poncho around her. Holes from dragging the firewood were patched to create a perfect vapor barrier. Then she would pull it over her head and sit, knees to chest, and breathe warm air over her body.

After an hour or so, the air would get stale and there would be too much condensation on the inside, so she would throw it off, leaving her face in the cold air, turn it over, and repeat the process. But even with the poncho and the jumper and the warm sand, the air temperature was dropping to the lower forties, maybe even the thirties. Her body shivered uncontrollably at times. Sleep did not come.

She wondered if the hallucinations would return, if she would have to fight for reality again in the cold of the night. One part of her wanted to hear her son's voice again. Another part kept a tight grip on the real world. Both parts of her mind wanted rescue—now. Why were they taking such a long time to find her? There were times when voices returned, mixing with the sound of water, but she turned them away. *If you can't be here in body, then don't bother coming in spirit*, she thought. *Stay away.*

Above her, the moonlight was shifting the shadows. The stars were coming in and out of sight. Clouds were gathering, and before long the quiet, soft rain came. Her poncho—her two-dollar poncho—and her jumper would keep her dry. The gift of the rain kept her from having to crawl again to the stream for a drink—another answer to prayer. She collected the drops in her poncho. It was cool and sweet, and she lapped her tongue in it. It was not alkali like the stream, but clear and moist and free. It was a comforting gift saying that she would be all right.

The rain brought a second gift. As the light crept into the canyon, the sage on the surrounding hills bloomed. The pollination poured into the little valley, sweetening the air. It was like a perfume factory. Victoria also took it as a sign that it would be a good day, and rescue was not far away.

A Day in the Sun

A shivering night sitting in a single position had worn a bedsore on Victoria's bottom. It was a distracting pain that could not be treated. She shifted around and began playing mind games to fight the boredom. She thought about women in other places, far parts of the world, whose acts of kindness had brought them into oppression and despair. *No one was looking for them. Their situations had no hopeful endings, but my situation will end. I will come home,* she told herself. The smell of sage and the quenching rainwater were poignant reminders of a time when she was younger and more prepared to be in this environment.

But she wondered and then wondered again why help had not come. Was it indifference? Incompetence? Had she moved out of a reasonable search area? She shifted her position to avoid the sore. Why had she survived so far? She had survived three nights out and two with a broken leg. Why was she okay? It was not her medical training. So far she had just given herself basic first aid. It was her mental training. So many times in her life—through Girl Scouts, through wilderness survival, through the canoe trip in Canada—she had asked herself what she would do in a situation like this. Now, in the face of death, in the face of survival, she wanted to fight, even if she did not win. But she would win, she told herself. Survival was not enough. The world wanted her back.

In time, she faded off to sleep again, warmed by the sun's rays and again confident that help would come. In the early evening, she ate the last of her snacks and drank a bottle of water. Her poncho that now enjoyed all the affection of a baby blanket was so full of holes that it leaked cold air. Her bedsore raged. Her leg throbbed. Her mind was cluttered. The temperature was dropping faster and further. On this night, the cold was coming quickly.

Every five minutes of so she would look at her watch and wonder how much longer she could endure.

It was about midnight when she stopped shivering. Stopped. She was still cold but no longer had the energy to shiver. She knew that was a bad sign. Fear knocked hard on the door. Death was standing right behind, and she realized for the first time that she could die that night—die alone in the red rocks, with words unsaid to loved ones, to her husband, to her son. It was the first time that she cried. It was the thousandth time she prayed.

But her will to live pumped on. She raised her hands above her head and began calisthenics. Gym class. Exercise to stay warm. Arms up, down. Fingers spread out. Stretch. Every five minutes she would do one minute of exercise. She was still cold and still not shivering. She wanted to shiver. She wanted the discomfort of the shaking, because she knew it was how her body created heat. Now her body was too close to hypothermia to expend energy shaking.

In the dark, quarter-moon night even the exercise could not keep her fully conscious. She faded into sleep, half hoping to hear the return of the imagined but comforting voices and images of the first night. Crazy made for good company. Rational thought meant she would be alone. Alone was hard. But the false images had always been far away, the voices distant and muddled by the stream. Now she was hearing something real and loud. Was this death? It chopped at the night. Then light flooded the little valley—hard and bright, blinding. Death was dark, not light. Loud noises. Big wind pushing down. A familiar sound. It was a helicopter flying low and slow. She could hardly see it in the bright light, but she could feel it on her skin, in her face. This was not a hallucination. It was real—close and present. She screamed, she yelled, she waved her poncho. Then it moved away. Surely they had seen her and were looking for a place to land. Then it came back, weaving and hovering.

But they had not seen her. The Utah Highway Patrol helicopter, which had been called in by a small county sheriff to make a hasty search, was just making a second pass through the creek bed as it searched the high-probability areas for a missing woman from Maine. They were less than thirty minutes into their search pattern and had seen nothing. But the experienced searchers knew that just because they had not seen Victoria did not mean that she was not there.

New York Calling

It was about that time that my pager went off. A small county sheriff in a place most would call nowhere needed support for his search. As one of the twenty members of Rocky Mountain Rescue Dogs, I was asked to provide K-9 search support for the trained volunteer searchers heading to the Escalante. A woman from Maine had failed to pay for her motel bill. Her car had been found at the Sand Creek trailhead. She had been missing, they thought, for four days, but the search was only now getting started. Even though I was stuck in a New York hotel, I knew that all over this little pocket of the west, several hundred people were asking their coworkers to cover for them, excusing themselves from family or social gatherings, grabbing a few food items, checking battery charges on radios, and then hopping in their cars and trucks to head for the Escalante.

It has never failed to fill me with awe. At a search site, an incident command center, trained searchers show up, one by one, each with a story about something important he left to help find someone he has never met and will never know. Searching is what we do. Finding is what we hope for. Helping is why we train. But in the vast spaces of western America, long roads between distant places and hard hikes take up most of the time.

Like many search "callouts," after paying the price of extracting ourselves from our regular lives, we received a "10-22" message—no longer needed. The 10-22 came to me several hours later in New York. Sorry I could not respond, I was curious about the circumstances. The 10-22 likely meant that the victim had been found. After being missing in the desert for four days, it was likely a recovery and not a rescue. Dead people give the wilderness a bad name. In this case, I was wrong.

Victoria lasted through the night on the false hope that she had been seen in the first flyover. In the morning, before sun poured again into her little valley, a pilot and a paramedic flew the same route again and again and then, finally, spotted her. They landed on the ridge above the valley, 250 feet from her camp. Her persistent faith, hope, intelligence, and resilience had earned her her heart's desire.

My Heart's Desire

When they landed, Victoria went into a momentary panic. What would they say? She assumed they had been looking for four days. They were probably tired and frustrated. Maybe they would be angry. She feared anger. "I'm fifty-eight years old, and I thought I would get the kind of lecture I got in the principal's office when I was six: 'What were you thinking?' 'Why did you...?' 'Do you know how much trouble you have caused?'" But instead, two big men in orange jump suits walked into her camp and asked, "How can we help?"

When I interviewed Victoria just thirty-six hours after the rescue, she described with great clarity how she felt when the helicopter descended. "It was like Christmas, like getting your heart's desire," she said. Victoria grew up a city girl in California, and every year, she asked for a pony for Christmas. "It was like getting the pony for Christmas after a long, long wait."

"I could hear them talking above me, gathering their gear, and climbing down the hill, through the hole and right to me. They were so nice," said Victoria. She could not remember all that was said, but she recalled the tone of their voices being so sweet. "I told them I was cold, and one of them took off his jacket and wrapped it around me. I was grateful for warmth—real warmth. I must have said something, because the other one took his coat off too and put it over me too." A double blessing, Victoria thought. There were no lectures. The pilot thanked her—thanked her for being alive and for her resilience. There were no questions except about her medical condition. Victoria knew quality care. "They put in an IV like complete professionals. They checked my vitals. Then they did an exceptional job putting on a splint."

In twenty minutes, the flying ambulance was in Panguich, Utah. On the way, Victoria thanked them for searching for so long. "I apologized for all the trouble of the four-day search, and they told me that the search had just started. I thought I heard them wrong."

The Second Trauma

Yes, Victoria thought, *I did not understand. Perhaps they had just come on shift while other searchers went off.* But in the hospital she spoke to her husband who clearly told her that they had only been searching since Friday night, less than twelve hours. "What? I told the motel clerk to expect me back at 9:30 p.m. on Tuesday, and the search did not start until Friday afternoon?" Victoria wanted to know what happened.

"It was such a shock to me. The whole time I was thinking that searchers were just around the corner or just over the hill, and they did not even know I was missing. My son, Ben, whose voice I had heard, did not even know I was gone. It violated my script.

It went against what I had been telling myself. When I realized I really could have died, the realization brought a second trauma."

The motel clerk, once off duty, had left for Colorado without communicating her plans to others. When her reservation expired on Friday and she failed to check out and pay, the motel owners called the sheriff. Upon entering the room, he found a bed that had not been slept in and a rental car contract on the desk. A quick search of local trailheads matched the contract to the car. The search began immediately, albeit three days after she had expected. All those times over the past three days when she had told herself that searchers were just around the corner—all those times—she had been lying to herself.

In Cedar City there was another trauma. The local media requested an interview, and Victoria reluctantly granted it. "I wanted to thank my rescuers," she said. "I wanted to thank those who brought me home." Within twelve hours, her story had gone national, and hundreds of reporters, and especially talk show producers, were offering to fly her to New York. "I just wanted to get home and get well," she said. Avoiding all publicity, she was back in Maine within a few days—back at home and back in the clinic. But for some reason, she returned my phone call and agreed to tell me her story. I am grateful. Her story has much to teach us about being lost.

The Unattended Alien

Hollywood movies teach us that the homecoming is the happy ending to the story. But coming home is never easy. For Victoria, nothing was the same when she got home. She had questions about the search and concerns about why the motel clerk had not reported her missing. "The worst day was the day after I got back. On the trip home, I started having more and more anxiety, fear of moving around and being so helpless, fear of what I would find when I returned home—everything. And on Sunday, I was feeling the kind of fear I've never had, which was fear of being afraid—fear that I would never feel safe and secure again. My mind kept going back to when I learned that no one had been looking for me."

It is not uncommon for us to create a script that we play over and over in our minds to bring us the hope and motivation needed to survive. Discovering that the script is fundamentally wrong can be as traumatic as discovering your "lostness." It is part of the persistence of post-traumatic stress and the resilience that emerges when people come fully face-to-face with their morality. Victoria persisted.

"I kept trying to find ways to talk myself through it. I told myself the world hadn't changed because of my experience. It was the same world, even if I felt like an unattached alien. It was only me that had changed, and now I could choose what I was changing into. I set myself little tasks to do and forced myself to do them. I prayed and read articles of religious encouragement and tried to get over feeling unworthy for help."

Like many who are lost and who come home, their anxieties persist until we can focus elsewhere. When we focus on being home and helping others, healing turns to wellness, persistence turns to resilience, and surviving turns to thriving. A new hope emerges, and our lessons learned while lost become treasures of life's wisdom.

Victoria shares, "I'm working on integrating all the parts of the experience into a meaningful and truthful whole that I can use as I return to the real world that I know wants me to come back. I can see myself as a *wayfinder*, using what I've learned to help others find their way. I still feel overwhelmed, but I can now imagine myself, having gone though this particular swamp, reaching back to help someone else move forward.

"Now I can see the angels in my life, people whose kindness is real and present. And I believe in myself now. It's only by believing in myself that I can move forward and move up. I have a deeper faith and hope."

Chapter 3:

Lessons

The wisdom of lost people contains powerful lessons that can help us know what to do when we become lost, help us welcome others home who have been lost, and, most of all, keep us from getting lost. This wisdom tells us how to stay closer to our communities, our families, and our rightful places. Four days in the wilderness changed Victoria forever. Each lost person who told his or her story for this book learned intensely while lost. Others could not tell their stories, but their learning can be extrapolated from their circumstances, experiences, and tragedy. For most, including myself, the telling of the "lost" story added new layers of understanding as I unraveled what I learned, why I survived, and what would have happened if I had done things differently. Gradually the pain, stress, and shame melted away, and what was left was wisdom. The wisdom can be summarized in nine lessons that are summarized in this chapter and detailed in the chapters that follow.

Lesson 1: Survival is insufficient.

The first lesson of the lost is that survival is insufficient. The "survival zone" is a place where you should spend as little time as possible. Survival establishes the minimum level of physical, emotional, and social needs that will deteriorate quickly. It is the tipping point between yes and no, making it or not, death and life. It is the point of maximum misery. Consider a desert survival situation where you have just enough water and food to stay alive. The heat during the day is paralyzing, the cold during the night overwhelming. One wrong move, one break from the shade or spill of the cup, and you pass the tipping point to death. Think of the stress of living in a place in work, life, or the wilderness where you are always looking over the edge, wondering if you might perish. Survivors need to move as quickly as possible into a position of thriving—at least in one area.

Victoria managed this concept brilliantly. The first night she took full advantage of the abundance of firewood, staying warm and thriving in a shelter. After breaking her leg on the second day, she didn't just try to get enough water to live; she tried for an abundant supply of water. She did not just sit and wait to be rescued; even with a broken leg, she built a fire, an ash bed, and a poncho shelter. To be sure, even with her moments of abundance, she came close to the tipping point, but without the warming fire on the first night and the abundant water from the stream, she would have never had the strength to endure the depravation created by the cold on the subsequent nights. Resilience is hard to develop in the survival zone, and the further you get from it, the more reserves you have. So following her own model learned through building a business, Victoria essentially created a savings account, not in money but in hydration, rest, and emotional and spiritual well-being. When she approached the tipping point, there were reserves to draw on. She said, "I learned a long time ago that success breeds confidence." Even the success of building a fire with a single match was something she celebrated.

Lost people who return home teach us that living in the survival zone is not sustainable. The longer you are there, the more you experience disruptive stress in an uncertain environment that could change at any moment. While everyone needs to learn how to survive, your goal should be to stay in the survival zone for as short a period as possible. Learn how to thrive again. But then believe that you will be found.

Lesson 2: Think differently to see differently. See differently to act differently.

Lost people no longer have a working understanding of the changed environment. Meanings have been disrupted, and the lost person is becoming overwhelmed with possibilities. The problem of being lost is not about having enough data; it is about having too much data and not enough useful information. Lost people find themselves in a state of meaning deprivation. What they think prohibits them from seeing what course they need to take in order to be found. A change in action requires a change in the way they see and think about their environment. Denial blocks this change. It is painful, but old notions created by the lost person's own successes and history need to be questioned and, in some cases, discarded. New relationships between the "lost" and the environment need to be formed. All of these begin in the person's head when he begins to think differently.

A firefighter lost in the Colorado Rockies spent several cold nights separated from his hiking companion. Lost but with a full pack, he followed the rules for no open fires in the forest. After several rescue helicopters flew near him, he changed his thinking:

I am not a firefighter in this situation; I am a victim. He built a fire, created smoke, and was rescued in a short period.

A retired professor who had been in the classroom for forty years lost his savings after a series of bad investments. Unable to teach anymore and unwilling to live just on his pension, he rethought his identity as a knowledge entrepreneur. While some in his family were skeptical, he started a small business in his basement. Over the next four years, he earned back his losses and more.

The second lesson of the lost is what the people in these examples did—think differently. *Thinking* differently allowed them to *see* differently and then act differently. The different thinking produced a different result. Being lost is a mental problem first. Victoria Grover solved the mental problem by making the best use of what she had. A jumper, a poncho, a pit fire, and a prayer were all ways of thinking differently, seeing things differently, and acting differently. Without this thinking, exposure and hypothermia would have taken her on the second or third night.

Lesson 3: See how others see you.

What would your parents say about your situation? Your partner? What would others tell you about how to see changes in the new environment? Lost people experience a sense of deprivation that leads them to a realization that they are lost. Deprivation is a poverty of spirit that creates shame. Shame isolates people. The lost person often tries to become less visible to protect his identity as a competent hiker, worker, or person. Driven by shame, in the early stages of lost, people are more likely to continue to cut themselves off from the important information they need to see themselves in the context of the new environment. If a person has physically separated and/or socially deviated to the point of being lost, then she no longer has a sense of place in the larger community.

Honest friends and family say where you went wrong, but it is hard to hear what they say. They will tell you when you separated from your community and when you deviated from your values. They will tell you how they experienced your being lost. Lost people who are found aid in the intervention by becoming more visible.

For example, a scout leader was lost in the Boundary Lakes Wilderness Area. At first he was angry, telling himself that he was not lost, and then got angry with everyone from the mapmakers to the Boy Scouts. His shame drove his feelings further and further away from reality. Finally, he asked himself how he would react as a searcher: "Where would they look for me? How could I be seen in this dense forest?" Just imagining how others would see him, helped him overcome the shame of his predicament. He returned to the one small opening that he had found in the trees, and within twelve hours, he was spotted by a rescue helicopter.

Shame is a destructive, isolating kind of fear—a toxic waste dump created when an old identity is shattered and a new identity is formed. It often hits the oldest harder, because they have professional or community-based identities that are formed over many years. I have seen several colleagues lose elections or retire. After the departure ceremonies and the thanks, they are alone and wandering. I met one such man in a store in Texas. He was a middle-aged man who had worked as an engineer for twenty-three years in the aerospace industry. Then he lost his job. He spent most two years looking for another engineering job, but he was always competing against younger people with fewer salary demands. Depressed after failing in one job interview, his anger spilled over to his family. In the heat of an argument his wife told him, "You are no longer an engineer. You haven't worked as an engineer for two years." Realizing she was right, he began rethinking who he was. He began selling some of his model airplane collection. Realizing this was a good source of revenue, he opened a small store and became one of the leading model airplane distributors in the region.

My friend had to let go of his identity as an engineer in order to find his way out of the unemployment wilderness. But part of you always stays left behind in the place of your life-changing experience.

Lesson 4: You are never lost alone.

In September 2012, I was called with my team to support a rural sheriff on a search for a fifty-six-year-old woman who had been missing in the Uintah wilderness area for twenty-four hours. Our team arrived at the trailhead of a well-traveled trail just a few hours after being called. The sheriff had set up a command post and brought in his own SAR team. Then he called others, like Rocky Mountain Rescue Dogs, to aid in the search. Still others who were in the area on horseback joined in. People from the nearest town thirty miles away began showing up to help, bringing food for the searchers and support for the impromptu town that now was too big for the parking lot.

At least two hundred searchers were mobilized on a Sunday morning, each of them a stranger to the subject but bound by the hours of training and the deep personal cost that comes with being a volunteer search-and-rescue worker. Just before dark, as the commander contemplated calling it off for the night, the woman was found. The searchers were called in, and the grateful subject, before going to be checked out at the hospital, went through the camp and thanked each of the strangers who had come for her.

In the early stages of being lost, you do not have a realistic understanding of the community that you have left, including who will help and how the help will come to the rescue. No one is ever lost alone. There is a network of people, some of them strangers, who will work to restore you to your life. Family, friends, spiritual advisors, coworkers—your entire social network—is profound. But when you are lost, people who don't even know you, who have been training for years in various professions, will try to find you, rescue you, and bring you home. All you need to do is reach for those who are reaching.

When I was a news reporter, I covered the story of a lost Boy Scout. Several hundred searchers had been looking for the boy for three days. The young scout had gone the wrong direction down a trail and continued hiking for ten miles. Eventually, no worse for wear, he was picked up by an elderly couple, fed a good meal, and returned to the camp. I was in the parking lot full of rescue workers, media, and worried family and friends when the couple pulled up and dropped the boy off. He wandered through the rescue camp with a puzzled look on his face. The rescue teams paid no attention, as they did not expect to find the victim in the parking lot that had become search headquarters. Finally, the young man saw his mother and said, "Hey, Mom! What are you doing here?" After a series of hugs and a quick checkup, the young man asked, "What are all these people doing here?"

Like many, he had no idea that friends, family, and strangers would mobilize to his aid. In order to be found, lost people need to realize that others might be searching for them.

In some cases, others realize a person is lost before he does. (I will discuss this more later in the book.) The parents of an alcoholic son or the wife of a drug-dependent husband are sometimes the first to alert someone to being lost. In other cases, people are lost for a long time before anyone realizes that help is needed.

For example, a recovering alcoholic who I interviewed for this book realized that his friends contributed to his problem. They continued to see him as a "drinking buddy" despite his efforts to stay sober. He also realized that the last time in his life when he had the important affirmation that supported a positive self-image was in high school. He cut relations with his destructive friends and reconnected with a few high school friends, including a high school teacher who became an important life mentor.

Norman Maclean wrote a beautiful and haunting novella called *A River Runs Through It* in order to make sense of his own brother who was lost in self-destructive behavior. Robert Redford made the book into a film by the same name. In the story, Maclean's younger brother, who was his father's favorite son, was killed over a gambling debt, breaking his father's heart. Maclean wrote, "It is those that we live with and love that we understand the least, but I still reach out to them." (MacClean, 1989) The human need to reach out is universal. Not everyone wants to be rescued, but we all want to rescue, and we do.

Lesson 5: Movement creates opportunity.

When you are lost, you can afford fewer mistakes. Inaction is not an option, but wrong-headed action can also be lethal. The fear of making another mistake can be paralyzing. There are two generic strategies—you must head in what you think is the right direction one step at a time, or you must hunker down, survive, make your situation better, and wait to be found. The first, or "hike out," strategy is the higher cost and higher risk strategy. The "hug a tree" strategy is more conservative and requires patience and a certain psychological fortitude. Either one of these can be the right thing to do, and either one can be fatal. Later in this book I will give examples of how both of these strategies were used and why they can be both right and wrong.

When sources are scarce, time becomes your enemy and you cannot afford to both "hike out" and "hug a tree." You must decide based on the best available information. If you are lost, you have already spent some resources (your ideas, stamina, food, shelter) on trying to be found. When you challenge yourself to renew your resources in the new environment—such as finding ways to make shelter, finding food and other essentials, or finding the right and best way down a mountain—you challenge yourself to learn. Learning always brings confidence and inner strength. So movement while staying put or traveling creates new information that brings clarity to a situation.

For example, a person who is lost in an unemployment line may be found as the volunteer in the community. There she finds connection, learning, and a new set of experiences. The action of moving forward in service translates into moving forward in a career. Another person whose career had stalled started running. "If I can't get the job I want, I need to do something I love," he said. In running, he met new people who shared his love of running, but some were good career connections. One day, after a long trail run with a group of new friends, he opened up a conversation with a fellow runner that led to a "dream job" in a different company. His movement eventually created an effective self-rescue strategy.

Lesson 6: Some small things matter; some big things do not.

A stable environment blinds us to both what is essential and what is not needed. Abundance dulls our ability to choose priorities over necessities. The gift of a rapidly changing environment is that it teaches us what is essential and what is luxury, what we need and what we do not.

In the wealthy neighborhood where I grew up in a modest household, some of my friends failed to build the foundations of education and discipline to be successful in their lives because their parents' wealth created the illusion of a safety net. They did not understand that as they dined with me as their guest at the country club and drove high-priced cars with me as their admiring passenger that they were losing their ability to see what mattered and what did not. They had never had to make a choice based on a priority, only on a preference. When the waiter at the country club asked whether they wanted the fillet or the catch of the day, they made a choice based on their preference. When their fathers asked them if their next car should be a Mustang or a Camaro, they made a choice based on preference. They had never had to make a choice based on a priority. Priority choices are small choices with big consequences. Made right, they can mean the difference between being lost and being found.

For example, in the now famous 2011 Sendai earthquake and tsunami in Japan, one woman carried her doll collection to safety but barely survived the lack of water and food for three days before rescue came. Many times during those three days she offered her dolls to others for the essentials. In the wilderness, so many times searchers follow a trail of discarded essentials only to find the body of a missing person clutching an item of high personal meaning but no practical value. In a stable environment, we lose the capacity to determine what is important because we do not have to make the forced choices that come in a rapidly changing environment. Knowing what matters is the first step in coming home.

Lesson 7: Fear itself can kill you.

Rita Chretien, who was lost for forty-eight days and whose story I detail later in this book, told me that her daily battle was not hunger or loneliness; it was fear. "Fear," she said, "would sneak up in the night" and surround the van where she was waiting for help. "But I didn't let it in."

While there is no doubt that fear can motivate, sustained fear stresses and attacks confidence, leaving victims blinded, less mobile, and unwilling to act. Fear comes in the form of self-doubt and tells you that you cannot save yourself. Fear comes in the form of shame and tells you that you are not worth saving. Fear comes in the form of an idea drought and keeps you ignorant and inactive. Fear can and does kill many victims.

Fear grips some families or organizations like a chokehold, giving them just enough oxygen to breathe but not enough to move. Fear of failure drives creativity underground or stomps it out all together. Fear of someone else's negative emotions drives honesty out. Fear of inaction or retaliation for wrong action leads to movement but not to progress. One manager, who I interviewed in a consulting project, described a work group he took over as so paralyzed with fear that they were splashing around making a great deal of noise but taking the enterprise nowhere.

Until you can purge your mind, your relationships, and your work environment of fear, you cannot find your way out. Blinding and binding fear can kill you—literally.

Lesson 8: No one is saved without hope.

People who are rescued but who have no hope will be lost again. The Wendover, Nevada, man whose remains we found had been lost for a long time. Rocky Mountain Search and Rescue and the

Wendover Sheriff's office were the first groups to officially search for him. A loving wife had tried to sustain him for years leading up to that day in the desert, but he had no hope. It was the lack of hope that led to his death.

Hope is a self-renewing fuel generated by positive social interaction. Hope for reconnection is what motivates the rescued and the rescuer. Hope drives the mind to see what was once unseen, the body to endure the unendurable, the soul to forgive, and the imagination to create. People who are rescued but have lost hope often go missing again. Hope is the acknowledgement that when we are in the hands of others we can be cared for and nurtured. Victoria Grover had an abundance of hope. Others do not.

When I began my volunteer search-and-rescue work, I assumed that I would mostly be finding lost children and reuniting them with their appreciative mothers. But almost half of our missions are known or possible suicides. On a cold Saturday in 2011, we were called to an island in the Great Salt Lake to search for a despondent man who was thought to be suicidal. Earlier in the year he had been the subject of a mountain rescue. He was released to his parents and a spiritual advisor who offered moderate help, but soon he had returned to the same self-destructive patterns. After a few days, he sank into hopelessness again, and within a week, he was once again the subject of a wilderness search. On the third search, we were called to the shores of the Great Salt Lake, where we found his body. Without hope, his self-destruction could not be contained. He never really came home after the first search.

Lesson 9: Found people are forever changed.

Most hope to go back to the ideal past, now filtered by memory. A traumatic lost episode will change all, but that does not mean a new, better future is not available. In Thomas Wolfe's novel *You Can't Go Home Again* (1940), protagonist George Webber realizes, "You can't go back home to your family, back home to your childhood ... back home to a young man's dreams of glory and of fame ... back home to places in the country, back home to the old forms and systems of things which once seemed everlasting but which are changing all the time—back home to the escapes of Time and Memory." (Shapiro 2006:883)

People who are truly lost are forever changed, sometimes by the hope generated in the newfound relationships and sometimes by the traumatic stress of "touching the void." You cannot expect to leave, be lost, and return the same person. In the same way, you cannot expect loved ones and others to be the same. Survival expert Laurence Gonzales describes the spiritual changes that happen when someone has been lost and are found. He says, "Survivors discover a deep spiritual relationship to the world. They often have a talisman to connect them with it, a sort of lifeline from inner and outer reality (22)."

For Victoria Grover, the aftermath of her survival experience was as difficult as the experience itself. Dealing with travel logistics, family, media, and her business in the hours and days after her rescue was a second trauma for her. She was still dealing with it months later. Victoria is not alone in her experience.

Being lost is a time of high learning.

The deep and valuable lessons that people learn while lost are often unrecognized or unspoken. Yet they are simple and built on a foundation of wisdom. In the coming chapters we will examine each of the lessons of the lost in greater detail. By now you have figured out that this book is not just about being lost in the woods; it is also about being lost and found in life. We have all been lost. Everyone has. But we have not all been found. If you are trying to come home or bring someone home, then please read on.

"Training to be on a SAR Team"
Use the QR code scanner on your smart phone
to watch a four-minute video by the author.
(Also available at LessonsoftheLost.com)

Lesson 1: Survival is insufficient.	Survival is what you do until you can find a way to thrive.
Lesson 2: Think differently to see differently. See differently to act differently.	Old solutions almost never work when you are really lost.
Lesson 3: See how others see you.	It has value even when they are wrong.
Lesson 4: You are never lost alone.	Someone will always come if they know where to look.
Lesson 5: Movement creates opportunity.	Constantly try to improve your situation.
Lesson 6: Some small things matter; some big things do not.	There is a new economy at play. Money may not matter but matches do.
Lesson 7: Fear itself can kill you.	Fear is a brick of toxic waste. Move away as quikly as possible.
Lesson 8: No one is saved without hope.	If you don't find hope when you are lost, you will return but still be lost.
Lesson 9: When you are found, you are forever changed.	You will never come home as the same person in the same place.

PART II: FOUND

Chapter 4:

Survival Is Insufficient

Winter comes like a thud in the High Uintah Mountains of Utah. The October storm at twelve thousand feet stung our exposed faces, sending us scurrying into our packs for hats, gloves, and jackets. The urgency of the screaming wind and horizontal snow amplified the precarious situation. Seven miles in and two thousand feet above a warm car and cabin, in a once familiar forest, we were lost.

Early that day contrasting autumn browns made direction clear. Within minutes, blowing snow and a sharp wind made everything the same shade of flowing white. The vast, clear horizons became blurred snapshots in a portable visual pocket of indistinguishable landscape. Boulders, trees, and paths were now dressed in raging white that made directions almost impossible. The inner storm was also growing. I felt an unfamiliar fear, a need to control panic, and unmitigated shame. I was lost in a whiteout with my friend Peter Robinson.

The best lessons happen in the wilderness. Wilderness lessons are brutally honest, are multidimensional, and happen in real time. Wilderness learning is not trapped within the artificial boundaries of disciplines such as psychology, sociology, or organizational studies. You cannot stand outside the wilderness and observe. You experience universal truth that is also immediate and personal. It is not confined to a particular social strata or theology. Wilderness learning is egalitarian, both immensely practical and deeply theoretical.

Once when I was crossing a high mountain meadow on a solo hike, like an Indian brave or a mountain man, my intuition told me to stop. The hair on the back of my neck was literally standing up. I was being watched. I knew it. I could feel it but not see it. I stood, scanning the trees surrounding the meadow. After five minutes, deep in the shadows of the trees I saw a dangerous animal—a bull moose. Even though the shadows obscured its features, I could tell he was looking right at me, ready to bound or defend based on how I moved. But how did I know he was there? What set off the alarm on the back of my neck?

Scholars of human behavior tell us that the environment offers more information than observers can process in real time. I had likely seen the shape of that moose and many other shapes as I entered the meadow, triggering feelings of intuition. It took more time to see with my rational eyes. Today I trust my intuition and give myself time to turn promptings into rational action. When a student comes with a "homework" problem, if I am still and look for shapes in the shadows, I can see other, more pressing issues. Then, sometimes, I can help at a deeper level.

Even more recently, when Dusty the Wonder Dog was just a puppy, I was hiking through a meadow, off-trail. As we approached a group of trees, Dusty went into an emphatic defensive alert. He barked but would not move closer to the trees. I looked. I could not see anything. I stood there for five minutes. He continued to alert, keeping me from moving closer to the trees, standing as my defender. Unable to see anything, I took a picture with my camera and then gave the trees a wide berth. "Trust your dog," I was learning from my search-and-rescue training. Trust your dog to see with his nose hundreds of details that you cannot see or smell.

When I returned to the cabin, I opened the picture I took on my laptop and zoomed in. After a few minutes, I found the shape of a bear's head, with eyes and snout visible. Trust your dog, I have learned. Sometimes the least among us see, hear, and know something that will save us.

Blinded by Ambition

Peter and I started our assent to the ridge that led to the summit of LaMotte Peak in warm sunshine, uncommon for early October. The days were shorter in this seasonal fringe time, so each morning the crusty ice that trimmed the river and stream banks was a little thicker. Usually by afternoon it was gone, leaving a few hours of almost summer. It was in this narrow window of opportunity, one day before the first major storm of the winter that we set off for the summit and a lesson in being lost.

The peak lay above us. The ridgeline lay beyond us. The trail lay before us. Wet grass that soaked the bottom third of our pant legs and the chill went intentionally unnoticed as we headed through the grass and into the trees. Soon the altitude and the deadfall slowed our progress. Our unmarked and unmapped route was familiar to me. Once in the aspen, we headed up enough to let the geography funnel us toward the small streambed that eventually became a steep canyon. There were signs in the deeper shadows of a snowfall weeks earlier, but even with the melt of the first minor snow, the stream would be dry at this time of year, and the trail leading up the canyon would be the easier option.

As we rose one step and one breath at a time out of the aspen, the forest turned to pine and fir. Our trail appeared on no map but had its own history. A hundred years ago, a hermit miner named Lee Christmas had led his mules up this canyon. Once the drainage became too steep for even mules, he cut a switchback trail to his secret mine shaft. The mules carried equipment up and ore down to the river, where we presume he washed it in hopes of finding the flakes of glitter that give hope and encourage further exploration.

We presume that he found something, because his efforts continued for twenty years. We also know that he, and many of the miners who explored these mountains, died with little or no fortune. From Spanish explorers to the Mormon pioneers and modern prospectors, the tales and trails of gold in the Uinta Mountains of Utah have made more people poor looking for gold than rich finding gold.

Still, as we sucked the thin air and stepped over downed trees, we were grateful for the persistent hermit whose daily routine one hundred years ago made our one-time adventure a little easier. Our goal was not gold or fame or any kind of record. Our goal was the summit of LaMotte Peak and with it pride and a sense of accomplishment that this middle-aged man craved.

By the time we reached the switchback, the excitement of the first steps had faded, and we were struggling to find the speed that would let us breathe and still make respectable progress. Just at the point where hands would be needed to go any farther, a cut veered east and out of the drainage. Up through the thick trees we trudged to our first open point, where the monument to Lee Christmas's dream lay as an open shaft, perhaps ten feet across and dropping straight down beyond sight. The edges of the shaft were precariously crumbling, and there was no fence or safety stops. Still, we could not resist taking a break and cranking our necks as far as we could over the edge to peer down in the blackness.

The full satisfaction of our curiosity would be a fatal mistake. The shaft was too deep and too crumbling for any safe exploration. So we turned our heads south to see just how far we had climbed. A thousand feet below, and perhaps a mile's worth of steps, along the dirt road in the meadow, we could see the car. There were no campers in the campground, no fishermen in the meadow, and no smoke coming from the rows of cabins near the bridge. It was late in the year, and the hunting seasons had passed, leaving the whole forest in anticipation of winter.

To the east, we could see Ostler's Peak, the darling of many a travel calendar. It is the most majestic of the peaks, towering over the Stillwater Fork of the Bear River that meanders through five miles of open meadow. We had picked LaMotte Peak because it is higher and less climbed than Ostler's, Hayden's, or even A-1 Peak to the south. On this day, it was not, however, majestic. It was just a lump of rocks along a ridge, like an overweight big brother, more massive but less noticeable than his smaller, younger brothers.

At the mine, we were a third of the way up the mountain. The second third included a pass by Scow Lake where I had camped many times. In my younger days, I might have been able to make it to Scow Lake before noon, but it was one o'clock in the afternoon before we made it, pausing only long enough to gobble some trail mix and take a long drink. From there, we could connect with the second weakened trail that led up to a second ridge and to the summit.

It was two o'clock before we made the second ridge. Now we were above the timberline. To the east, we could see a full view of the Uintah Mountain Range, with a clear view of Kings Peak, the thirteen thousand-foot-plus peak that is Utah's highest. To the north, we could see the Wind River Range in Wyoming.

Just beyond the horizon was Gilbert Peak, Wyoming's highest. Between the Wind River Range and the Uintahs were the plains of Wyoming, severed down the middle by the ribbon of black that we call I-80. We had a high-altitude view of humanity. We could see the farms and ranches but not the houses, the rails and roads but not the trains and tracks.

But to the south we enjoyed no such view. The winter storm expected later that night was bearing down on us. The black, boiling clouds of this weather front lined the horizon. We were almost to twelve thousand feet, on an open ridge, staring a monster in the face.

At first view of the wicked weather, we picked up the pace, hoping to outrun the onslaught to the summit. While Peter was more prudent, I produced a deliberate ignorance of what might happen to us after the summit. For years, I had seen LaMotte Peak towering over the meadows that were the playground of my youth. I had climbed many peaks around LaMotte, but it always looked down on me. I had tried once by myself but gave in when it became clear I could not get past the snow bridge without gear and anchoring companions. This late in the year the conditions seemed perfect. We had paid the price to get this far. I was up for the adventure and wanted to have a bragging story for my friends.

"We can make it to the top and come down in the storm," I told Peter.

That made a lot of sense to me at the time. We had all of the gear needed for the climb. We were experienced. I had been in many storms before. But my companion Peter Robinson is a thoughtful scholar/practitioner psychologist who studies entrepreneurs. He is trained to evaluate how others perceive risk. He knew that I was ignoring my environment, denying my senses, and focusing too heavily on my goals. He knew what I proposed was too risky. Still, I insisted. I wanted to get to the top.

White Right Jab

The storm hit like a boxer hitting a jaw. One minute it was a beautiful sunny fall day. The air was crisp, and the aspen leaves had turned from yellow to orange to brown. For a while, there was a pregnancy in the air that stirred my awareness, and I knew all this calm and beauty would be swept away in the moment of the first storm.

With reluctance, we turned and headed down from the second ridge to Scow Lake. In the thirty minutes it took us to get from the ridge to the lake, the conditions changed dramatically. There was a whole new attitude as the environment went from peaceful to intense. The wind blew the snow directly into our faces. Visibility dropped from miles to feet in just a few minutes. What had been a beautiful color pallet of fall colors was now black and white—mostly white.

We crossed the meadows east of the lake. Since we had left the old mining trail, we had followed my sense of direction. Now in the whiteout, it was obvious that we could easily become disoriented. But my mental map told me that if we got to the south side of the lake, we could go uphill to the first ridge and follow the ridge west until we came to the drop-down point where we would encounter Christmas's trail.

After passing the lake and struggling over snow-covered deadfall, we made our way to the ridge. In the thick pines, the wind was less intense, but we could see the tips of the trees being whipped by the wind.

When we reached the ridge, we turned right and began following along the point, keeping the downhill portion on our left. At times, we could only see twenty feet in front of us, so we watch carefully for the drop-down point for the miners' trail. After about thirty minutes, I was convinced we were getting close to the drop-down point. After another thirty minutes, I was concerned we might have overshot the drop-down point. Because of my overconfidence, created by familiarity with the terrain, we had no map, no compass, and no GPS.

We continued, but my instinct told me something was wrong. Like the bull moose and the snow bridge, my inner compass told me we were going the wrong direction. My eyes told me we were following the ridge, keeping downhill to the right, yet my intuition said were going the wrong direction. Then what I saw confirmed my fears. There were burnt trees on the left. They were on the left going up; they were supposed to be on the right.

My first thought was a form of denial. "Don't those stupid trees know where they are supposed to be? They're supposed to be on the right."

We stopped. I voiced my first concerns to Peter, but there was no urgency in my voice—just confusion. At first it was like someone was playing a joke on us that we would figure out after a few minutes. It could not be real.

"What if we were lost?" I joked bringing up the possible headlines: "Confused Professors Lost on Icy Mountain."

We imagined the quote in the local paper from our boss: "Between them they had twelve years of graduate school, but they were still too stupid to bring a compass and a map on a day hike, so they couldn't find their car in a little snow storm. We will miss them."

Then I began to imagine my students being relieved that our demise in the wilderness excused them from upcoming midterms. Some would be dancing through the halls singing, "Ding, dong, the witch is dead, which old witch, the wicked witch ..."

Joking is often a form of denial.

Peter said, "Let's just keep going. We have the downhill to our right, so we'll hit the trail sooner or later."

"Okay," I grunted.

After what seemed like a long time, it was not so funny anymore. The snow was thick, wet, and still blowing. Then it turned crystalline and cold. The wind stopped gusting and became steady, pushing the tops of the trees back with ease. The noise intensified and so did my emotions.

I have been in worse whiteouts, I thought. I remembered a time while doing a solo winter hike on snowshoes. The forgotten goggles made seeing in the wind and white almost impossible, but I had followed my own fading footprints back to the car just before they were eliminated altogether. I had always made it out with a good tale to tell friends and family who listened politely but were never really fully interested.

In this whiteout, on this adventure, pushing on was a good plan. Besides, what else could we do? It was too early to find shelter. And the shelter option was questionable. What if we were just a few feet from the drop-down point? What if this was just a quick storm, over in an hour? We would be foolish weathering out the storm on the mountain in those conditions.

We pushed on with these questions and a thousand more swimming in our minds, like a fast-motion silent movie that moves from scene to scene before you can digest what has happened. After about ten minutes, I hit what I now know to be the point of realization. This is the psychological point when people admit to themselves that they are lost. While a more detailed definition of this point comes later in this book, I will say that every lost person who I interviewed knows this point. It is the point that you say to yourself, above everything else, that you know you are lost.

The point of realization releases an avalanche of ideas, and feelings hit. I was in the woods with warm clothing, good equipment, an emergency shelter, and potentially warming fuel all around me. I had two days' worth of food in my pack, but I was blind to my relative abundance. I felt a poverty that evoked the fear of hunger and lack of shelter. I was without place and without means. My identity as a competent climber and hiker was now in question.

I had family and friends who I knew would search for me. Yet I felt the poverty of loss of affiliation. I felt alone in the world without connection or network. I also felt a poverty of identity. I had come into my adventure as a competent man, trained and experienced in wilderness survival and human behavior. But suddenly I was no longer an experienced expert, a guide, and an advisor. I was inept, incompetent, and ashamed.

"Stop, Peter." I said. "Somehow we got turned around; if we keep heading in this direction, we will be back at the lake in a few minutes, only we won't be able to see it."

Peter stopped. I could see that Peter was experiencing some of the same trauma that I was. He realized that we were in trouble. We could not afford another mistake, so whatever we did next, it needed to be the right thing.

We stopped under a tree, somewhat sheltered from the wind. There was a long silence, and then we started asking questions: "What do we have in our packs?" "Do you have a compass or a map?" "What do we have to build a shelter? "Who knows where we are?" "How will they react if we don't get home tonight?" I love to hike solo, but never before had I been so grateful for a companion. Peter pulled out some chocolate, and we munched a bit. Then we drank. The food and water break reminded us that our basic needs were not far away in our backpacks. Peter, a religious man, said, "I want to pray." So we did.

Out of the Survival Zone

In every environment, when people are lost, water is the first item needed for survival. Humans can go three minutes without air, three days without water, and three weeks without food. Air is part of every wilderness, whether desert or mountains, so water is our first physical need. But meaning is our first psychological need when we are lost. Unlike water, it is something that, for better or worse, we can make. When we start self-manufacturing meaning, we can go from an inconvenient lost to a critical lost as we sink deeper into our own emotional pits. The inner and outer compass is broken.

We often think new technology can protect us from being overwhelmed with equivocality. Technology has replaced road maps with GPS systems, but GPS technology, like any technology, can provide more data, yet, sometimes less useful information. Technology may help us find a more compatible mate, but it cannot help us manage the relationship. Technology can bring us more instantaneous financial data, but it cannot predict future market behavior. Technology does not protect us from being overwhelmed with equivocality; sometimes it even enhances our sense of being overwhelmed by too much information and not enough meaning.

Peter and I stood there on a mountain not knowing where we were, where we should go, or what we should do. Our mental map had collapsed and was replaced first by denial and then by a flood of questions. Were there other burnt trees that we had not known about? Were we going in the right direction? If we were going in the wrong direction, would we end up down the wrong drainage miles from the car? Had we overshot the drop down? Undershot? All of these were plausible. Fueling the problem were the external factors: what will my family, our colleagues, and our friends think when they see that we were lost?

If you have been lost in the wilderness, or lost in life or work, you have had similar feelings. The point when you realize you are lost might be related to your career, a job loss, an important relationship, or finally facing self-destructive habits. You ask why this is happening. Who can help? What should I do next? What will others think? The questions snowball, but the answers are hard to come by. At the intersection of psychology and organizational studies are ideas that might be helpful in understanding this condition.

Being lost is not just being in the wrong place at the wrong time; it is first a mental or psychological problem. When we are lost, we are often overwhelmed by uncertainty and deprived of meaning. Wilderness survival experts often talk about the priorities of survival. Water, shelter, and food are seen as the priorities. There are numerous popular books and media programs that teach people how to make a shelter, find a meal, or build a fire in an unusual circumstance. Similarly, there are numerous books and media programs that describe how to survive difficult economic times, retool your career, kick addictions, and live through changes in relationships. These are helpful and incomplete.

Survival is what you do until you have a plan for recovery. Recovery means you have learned to manage the uncertainty, found enough meaning to move forward, and are no longer in a state of equivocality. Peter's prayer took us out of the state of equivocality. It opened our minds to a simple logic. If the burnt trees were on our left, then we had been turned around and were now heading the wrong direction. To confirm this, we only needed to turn right, hike over the ridge point, and see if we could find our tracks. We did, and we followed our tracks in the snow to a knoll. The snow had cleared a bit, and we could see how we had followed the contour of the knoll around and started back in the wrong direction.

Understanding our problem was just the first step in solving our problem. We continued along the ridge, looking for the drop-down point that was now hiding under a few inches of sticky snow. We dropped onto the miners' trail and followed it into the thickening clouds, breaking through just before we reached the shaft. At this lower altitude, the snow was a slushy rain that somehow found its way through anything waterproof and into my bones. Still, I was euphoric—euphoric and ashamed. We were lost and had been found. But we had been lost.

Total Recall

I could have put my experience in the place where you put other painful memories like that turbulent flight, the first breakup with a girlfriend, or a bad trip to the dentist. My thirty minutes of being lost on the mountain could have been reclassified as stress-related panic, and self-forgiveness and then forgetfulness would follow. But this experience was also rich as wilderness learning.

As we descended on the old miners' trail past the shaft, where tired mules hauled hopeful ore, I began writing this book. I thought of the other times I have been lost, most of them when I was not in the wilderness.

I have also felt lost at the death of loved ones, at the point of a career crisis, and when relationships change. Every one of these experiences had several things in common. First, the environment changed, and changed dramatically. A storm came. The trains stopped. We moved. What once made me successful in my career was no longer making me successful. Sometimes it's just a collection of small events that lead you off the path of certainty just one step at a time. You look around your family, your workplace, and your community, and nothing is familiar. You don't know which way to go to get home.

Survival expert Laurence Gonzales details the transformational stages that individuals go through when they experience radical changes in their environment and become "lost." (Gonzales, 2004) The stages resemble the steps identified by Elizabeth Kubler-Ross in her pivotal work on dying, commonly referred to as "The Five Stages of Grief." (Kubler-Ross, 1990) First, Gonzales says you deny that you're disoriented and press on with growing urgency, attempting to make your mental map fit what you see. This is exactly what Peter and I did as we decided to "press on." Then you realize you're genuinely lost, and the urgency blossoms into full-scale survival emergency. Clear thought becomes difficult as emotions swirl and rationality becomes illusive. This is the state when Peter and I began to be meaning deprived. Then, as equivocality overwhelms, actions becomes frantic, unproductive, and even dangerous. Often people in this stage form a strategy for finding some place that matches the mental map, but the strategy fails to resolve the conflict, so they see themselves running out of options and become resigned to their plight. Aside from confusion, a lost person suffers from a destructive synergy of forces, including exhaustion, dehydration, hypothermia, anxiety, hunger, and injury. Echoing Dr. Viktor Frankl, holocaust survivor and author of *Man's Search for Meaning*, "once psychological disintegration occurs, death is not far away." (Frankl, 2006)

If these ideas sound familiar to you, then you have been lost. I think if we are honest with ourselves, we will see that we have all been lost. These times when we were lost are times when we may feel victimized by a changing environment, by changing relationships, and by changing conditions. If we learn how to find useful meaning in the cloud of equivocality produced by changing conditions in work, life, or the wilderness, home and hope are one step closer. Of course, this means we need to face our understanding and knowledge, and honestly acknowledge our ignorance and vulnerability. This is why the lessons we learn while lost are among our most poignant and precious.

Chapter 5:

Think Differently to See Differently; See Differently to Act Differently

Kenny Blake was used to spending long days in dark places. As a coal miner in the Wilberg Mine in Orangeville, Utah, he was part of a team of eighteen miners who were trying to break a long-held long wall coal mining record. If they were successful, they would receive a patch for their safety jackets and a one hundred-dollar bonus.

By all accounts, Kenny was a keen observer. Even though he was not the most experienced person in the mine, he was one whom many looked up to—a thinker. As a friend put it, he had "the sense" to stay safe in what is a very dangerous industry. So when the coal conveyor belt stopped just before the end of his shift, Kenny took a long look up the wall and saw smoke.

It was six days before Christmas in 1984, and I was just drifting off to sleep when the phone rang. It was not unusual for me to get calls at all hours of the night. I had yet to discover the world of academics and consulting. I was working as the Central Utah Bureau Chief for KUTV News in Salt Lake City. "Bureau

Chief" was an impressive title in a job that was half glory and half pay. My assignment had me covering more geography than all the other eighteen reporters put together. I spent a lot of time in cars and helicopters. My job required that I have connections in all the small counties in central and southern Utah, regularly calling the police and sheriff's dispatchers to check in.

These daily and nightly phone calls that usually led to nothing paid off, because when the big news that television audiences liked broke in my area, the dispatchers would call me. I learned to have coherent conversations in the middle of the night about burning barns or lost dogs and only wake up when the dispatcher spoke key works like "fatal" or "plane crash." So I always listened, never cut the calls short, collected a few interesting recipes and gossip, and got good news stories.

On this night, it was the Carbon County Dispatcher who said, "A woman called me and said her husband went to work at the mine tonight and didn't come home." Before I could wake up enough to consider how much this was not a news story, the dispatcher said, "Scott, this is a big one." She gave me the name of Janice Carter and suggested I give her a call.

Half asleep, I gave Janice Carter a call. She told me that her husband was supposed to get off work at ten o'clock that night. When he was not home by eleven thirty, she called the mine, and the supervisor told her something was wrong. She did not know what to do. Somewhere in our conversation she spoke the key words that woke me up.

I cleared my mind enough to call the Wilberg Mine in Orangeville, Utah, but did not get an answer—curious. On almost any night, there would be someone there to answer the phone. I called Savage Brothers headquarters in Orangeville, which operated the coalmine for Utah Power and Light. When a person answered, I said, "This is Scott Hammond from KUTV

News—" Click. The person hung up on me. I called the mine again. This time I got an answer with a blaring alarm in the background. When I identified myself, the person at the other end said, "Can't talk," and hung up.

I called the news desk dispatcher at KUTV and arranged for a photographer to meet me at the freeway, and the two of us headed south. It was one o'clock in the morning and snowing hard.

The Tunnel at the End of the Light

By the time I was in the car headed for a three-day, 24/7 news coverage ordeal, Kenny Blake was safe, but twenty-seven of his colleagues were not. After Kenny had seen the coal conveyor stop and saw smoke, he went on a frantic search for breathing equipment.

"It came in pretty quick," he said. "As soon as it was there, it was thick."

Blake was unable to find the self-rescuers, but two fellow workers he encountered coming through the smoke handed him one of three rescuers they were carrying.

"I told them we should do something now," Blake said. "There wasn't time to stand around and argue about it. At that point, I couldn't see anything."

Blake tried to follow Tom Hirsch, a veteran miner who was highly respected. "He told me to call my insurance company," Blake recalled. But after a few minutes, "I lost Tom in the smoke. I didn't know where he was."

With coal smoke and blackness all around, it is no wonder that Kenny became disoriented, but he pushed forward, feeling his way with hands along the wall through a part of the mine he did not know. Along the way he came to various doors that he hoped would take him out of the smoke, but they were hot to the touch, so he kept moving. When he finally found a door that was not hot, he opened it up and stepped through, continuing to walk. "I could hear the fire, so I turned around and headed the other direction," Kenny said. "It [the fire] was roaring. At that time, I didn't know where I was." Kenny said the light from the fire was the only thing he could see, and the heat seared his clothing. Then he came across some firemen fighting the fire, and they pointed him to a mile-long, dark tunnel that led out of the mine. When he asked them about other trapped miners, the firefighters told him he was the only one they had seen.

When I arrived at the mine that night, we could only see past the gate to the hillside, illuminated by the snow. A steady alarm pierced the night, and smoke poured from the entrance like a dragon between breaths. I could not imagine a living thing inside that inferno. I spent the next three days sorting out this story and the next thirty years haunted by it. For the first eight hours, I was the only reporter in America providing coverage to everyone. Within twenty-four hours, there were more reporters in town than local residents. The story of Kenny Blake recounted to one of my colleagues gave wives like Janice Carter hope that her husband would return safely. On the night of December 22, just before the bodies of the twenty-seven miners were found, Janice came to me and asked if we could videotape the letters her children had written to their father. The first began "Dear Daddy, please come home for Christmas ..."

Why was Kenny Blake home for that Christmas and the many that have come since, and the others were not? He was lucky, yes. He was smart, yes. But Kenny Blake had a series of wayfinding behaviors that others did not. He saw differently, he thought differently, and so he acted differently. Unlike other miners, Blake went on alert when the conveyor stopped. It could have been routine, but he looked for smoke. When he saw it, he started thinking immediately about finding a self-rescue breather. When he was given one, Blake moved quickly to the next problem. "We need to get out now," he told the others. He knew the window of opportunity was closing fast. Blake persisted, even moving past the fire and the hot doors, while others did not or could not. He could hear and feel the fire, but he kept moving. In an interview just after the escape, he said, "I thought they were following me, but one by one, they dropped off until I was alone."

Being the only survivor of a major coal mining disaster does not feel heroic when your friends and comrades are left behind. I have no doubt that Kenny has suffered through survivor's guilt and even some resentment in the small mining town that he calls home. Most "lost" situations require you to act in a different way. New information demands a new series of ideas and actions that are not covered by the unusual routine. Old notions created by your own history and even successes need to be questioned and, in some cases, discarded. Kenny did that, and he lived.

Author's Note: In December 2012, just a few days before Christmas, I was called with my Rocky Mountain Rescue Dogs team to Orangeville to search for a missing man. Not much had changed to make that tiny community look different from almost thirty years ago. The close-knit local SAR team all knew the subject who had been struggling with drug abuse for years. They were absolutely professional in their approach to the search and deeply appreciative of our support. Unfortunately, our efforts yielded nothing, and the case remained open at the time of publication of this book.

Wayfinding People

Dogs are better than humans at finding lost people, not because the dogs are smarter but because they are simpler. They have a nose that smells at the same level our eyes can see. When commanded to "find," the search dog's mind does not bring up a long history of experiences or a series of historical conceptions that may be wrong. A dog just simply uses his nose to follow the scent to the source.

When Dusty is working a wilderness or area search problem, we have a definable space to clear. The most common strategy is to make a cut through the area at the farthest downwind point. When the dog raises his nose into the wind like he is trying to catch something, then you know that he has a scent. The scent is a trail of microscopic skin rafts coming off the victim. Most often, the search dog will simply turn into the wind and follow the scent to its source. Even though I have seen it hundreds of times while training, it is still amazing to see Dusty's nose go up, his tail start to wag in excitement, his direction change to a straight line, and the victim found.

Humans are much more complicated than dogs. In recent years, psychologists, urban planners, communication theorists, and a number of other types of scholars have examined "wayfinding" behavior in adults. Urban planner Kevin A. Lynch first used the term in his 1960 book called *Image of the City* where he said, "wayfinding is a consistent use and organization of definite sensory cues from the external environment." (Lynch, 1960) Kenny Blake responded to sensory clues deep in the Wilberg mine. In his mind, he could see a pathway to an exit. He could also see that soon the path might be blocked with fire, so he moved quickly "without argument."

Wayfinding behavior also includes human interaction with symbols—a hot door, a warning sign, and a subtle or obvious change in the environment. While much of the research of this new science has been conducted in urban or virtual environments, it is immensely useful in understanding how we make our way through work, life, and the wilderness.

Wayfinding skills have evolved in humans over thousands of years. Hunters and gatherers relied on wayfinding not just to find prey, but also to bring the spoils of the hunt home after a long journey. Wayfinding traditions have been documented in indigenous cultures that did not have the technology to navigate, yet were immensely successful in taking long journeys. Polynesian seagoing canoes traveled from island to island in the world's largest ocean using only wave patterns to determine direction of travel. Bedouin tribes in the ocean of sand that spreads across northern Africa can determine the right way to go by looking at the shadows that come off the large sand dunes. While the small dunes move with each storm, the large dunes, sometimes two hundred feet high, follow the prevailing winds. Following these patterns gives the leader a sense of the way across a desert that has no visible landmarks and no vegetation.

In modern times, humans have come to rely on technology to direct them. Having a GPS, map, and compass overrides the need for environmental clues. Still, some have a hardwired need to know where they are. I am one of those people. Years ago I gave up the convenience of an aisle seat on a plane in order to watch the geography out the window. I watch the mountains, the rivers, and the position of the sun to tell where I am and how much longer the flight will be. I am more relaxed and more comfortable when I can see the horizon and know my direction of travel. More than once my sense of direction has caught another searcher's misread of a GPS, map, or compass direction.

Unlike dogs, humans are largely visual and conceptual in their sensemaking. We are visual because we use sight to determine what is going on around us. This is why Kenny Blake's story is so amazing. He engaged wayfinding behavior without being able to see the way. We are constantly looking around and seeing the exits, the way to the open parking place, the next stop on the subway, or the way home. Just like any animal on the plains or in the jungle, we look for security, familiarity, and comfort. But what we do next is what really makes us human.

Any animal can use eyes, nose, ears, or a combination of those to see and map its immediate environment. But only humans connect what they see with what is beyond the horizon or out of sight. We conceptualize or imagine how our seeable environment is connected with the larger world. It is that ability to conceptualize and connect that gives ordinary people great careers, helps families go farther than they could ever imagine going on their own, and helps Kenny Blake find his way out of a burning mine.

When you get to the part where you are no longer able to see, no longer familiar with the territory, you need to conceptualize where you are. Psychology gives us terms like *situational awareness* and *sensemaking* that are important concepts in understanding how we think through the conceptual leap. But it is a simple lesson: we are better wayfinders when we can connect the path that we can see with the path that we cannot see.

Can you connect the meeting that you are in with your career and the future of the company? Can you connect the school or special training that you are paying for with your future career? Can you connect the conversation you are having with you partner with the future of your relationship? Can you see how your behavior as a manager, parent, leader, or teacher is being woven into the lives of others? Can you see how your next step down this path will lead to another path and then out of the woods?

Sometimes the window for action is so narrow that there is not enough time to give a full rational explanation until the event is passed. But if you can connect and act, you might walk out of a burning mine when no one else can.

King's Peak Promise

At ten thousand feet, the blue sky feels like it is close enough to touch. Standing at Henry's Lake, I watched the morning sun stretch the shadows of the tall trees across a ragtag group of tents. I was the first to awake in our group of about thirty adults and scouts who were camped at the base of King's Peak, Utah's highest mountain. I was looking forward to the 3,500-foot assent to the summit that day. I had tried it twice before in my younger years, and both times weather had pushed me back. As the only east-to-west mountain range in the United States, the Uintahs capture the summer thunderheads nurtured on the plains of Wyoming with a predictable twenty-minute deluge almost every afternoon.

This was a day beyond beauty. The overnight rain had cleansed every particle from the atmosphere, creating the sense that you could touch heaven. The crisp air and the cracking of the wet firewood only added to the ambiance that Eden was just around the corner.

Unlike most of the scouts and adult leaders in the group, I had a simple pack—a rainproof tarp, a sleeping bag, and a simple stove to expedite boiling water for hot chocolate and instant oatmeal. I was done with breakfast before most were out of their sleeping bags, so I loaded my pack and then told the leaders that I would meet them at the top of Gun Site Pass.

The trip up Kings Peak had three steps. The first was a long and relatively flat hike out of the tree line and up a long, closed valley. At the end of the valley there is a switchback trail leading to Gun Site Pass. The second step followed the ridge to Anderson Pass at about twelve thousand feet. The third step goes from Anderson Pass to the summit at 13,400 feet. I would go the first way on my own.

As I hiked along the valley floor, the day was beginning to mature, with the direct sunlight and dew highlighting the intense green with an occasional sparkle. At that altitude, it was still spring, and wild flowers were in full bloom. I remembered a poem by Harrison R. Merrill about these mountains that beings with "Dear God, let this be heaven."

Once I hit the switchback, it was all rocks. The red sandstone of the Uintahs had been cleared by the Forest Service crews to make this wilderness freeway that took three or four scout troops every day to the summit of Utah's highest peak. The sky looked like a blue canopy stretching from every horizon. As I rose up the switchback, I could see the plains of Wyoming. I could see the China Meadows Trailhead and the string of lakes we had hiked in the previous days. Behind me I could see all the way to Colorado. At Henry's Fork Lake, I could see a scout troop starting out on their summit quest. Because the tents from our troop were just coming down, I assumed it was one of several troops on their way to the summit. The only part of the 360-degree panorama that I could not see was to the southwest.

I took off my backpack and settled in for the long wait. As I watched the lead scout troop snake their way up the valley, I noted that the winds changed direction. It was ever so slight, but instead of coming from the northwest, the breeze was now coming from the southwest. Before long, the lead troop vanished below me; no doubt they were strung out along the switchbacks that I could not see from my perch.

The blue inverted bowl that framed my scene was cracked by a single cloud coming from the southwest. I remember thinking it seemed weird" without knowing what was weird. Then two young men appeared on the trail, leading out the first troop. "Where you headed?" I asked, though I knew what the answer would be.

"We're headed to the top," they said with confidence.

As others followed, my mood went from excited to emphatic. "We are not going to the top today," I told the next pair of boys. "Our troop is not going."

I was surprised when I said it. I did not know why. Besides, I did not really have the authority to make such a decision on behalf of thirty others, and I didn't have a presentable reason. But the moment I said it I knew it was right, and I picked up my backpack and headed back down the switchback.

When I met my troop at the base of the switchback, I held the boys who were leading out until the scoutmaster caught up. Then I made the announcement. "We are not going to the top today. The conditions are not right."

"You're kidding. Who are you to tell us?" The words were fast and furious. Everyone had summit fever. By then the environment had changed a bit, but it still did not support my point of view. The southwest wind had brought a collection of high clouds that was obscuring 50 percent of the sky. "It's not going to rain!" piped in one boy.

"You brought me because of my experience in these mountains," I said. "Now I don't really know why yet, but this is not the right day." The incredulous scoutmaster had a PhD in physics. He lived in a data-driven world. Intuition, impression, and hunches were not rational ways to make a decision, but to his credit he said, "This is a chance to learn to follow our leader. Turn around, boys."

With our sights on the tree line, we headed back. Within a few minutes, the first wall of wind hit us. It was a mighty gust that reminded us how quickly the world can change above ten thousand feet. Wind, rain, and then hail—visibility had dropped to two hundred meters. The wildflower meadow that I had hiked through two hours before was a swamp. The boys stopped to put on ponchos, but the blowing nature of the rain made those open garments almost ineffective.

Halfway down the meadow, things went from bad to worse. Up until this point, we had been uncomfortable. Now our lives were in danger. I first noticed that the hair on the back of my wrist started to tickle. Then I heard a crack and a boom, like a cannon shell at close range. A second one came thirty seconds later. Some of the boys headed toward the lone tree clump that had managed to grow above timberline. "No!" I yelled. "Stay away from the trees!"

Urgently, the leaders held the boys, sending them fifty steps apart down the trail. If lightning were to strike, we didn't want multiple casualties. The booms and flashes were more intense now. The air was full of electricity, and we could feel it. Our ears stung from the noise. Our eyes were dulled by the constant flashes. The rain turned to hail and then back to rain. One by one, we headed to the lower lakes, hoping to get out without getting hit.

At Dollar Lake we found a campsite in the rocks away from the trees. The lightning stopped, but the storm continued, making fire building difficult. Most of the boys settled into a soggy tent with their friends and a deck of cards. The next day they would walk out defeated by the mountain with a story of retreat to tell worried parents.

I had a different problem. Some parents had planned to meet us early in the morning as we came down the trail by Red Castle. I needed to continue to hike out and intercept those parents so that we would not miss them. After seeing everyone settled, I headed down the trail.

After hiking about an hour in the rain and the low cloud ceiling, I heard the rhythmic chop of helicopter blades. Within seconds, it passed over me, but I could not see it through the dense cloud cover. The helicopter noise told me two things. First, a rescue was underway, and second, they would only be flying in these conditions if there were a life-threatening situation.

Four scouts from another troop were huddled under a tree when lightning struck. Two were killed. My boys were safe in an area with less exposure.

What was I thinking? What did I see? It took a long time to figure it out and give a process to what I first thought to be just my imagination. After a lot of introspection, I realized that it was the southwest wind that had first triggered my alarm. Southwest winds in the Uintah Mountains in the summer are almost always weather fronts and not isolated thundershowers. It was also the shape of the leading clouds. I could not see the weather front, but I knew it was coming because of the shape of the clouds. I did not have the meteorological jargon or the rational explanation, but I did know the urgency of acting in the right way even though I have not yet figured out why.

This kind of preconceptual acting is what athletics is often about. You shoot, catch, block, or defend not based on a rational or intentional idea but on an instinct. You see a familiar pattern in the other team or in your opponent, and you exploit the advantage or minimize the disadvantage. If your game is serious, your coach plays film later, and retrospectively, you are able to think about your thinking and see the pathways where action was supported by your conceptualization.

Pathway to the Conceptual

All right paths begin with a real place and lead into the imagination. All real problems begin in the present and lead into the future. They lead us to the imagined and future safety, the imagined and future career success, or the imagined and future happiness. But not all stories end as we imagine. It is our ability to see and understand our current environment and then conceptually connect it with a realistic ideal in the future that is the first lesson of the lost. Some are blinded by the current reality. They are familiar with the status quo, and so they hold on to it even when it may be killing them. They will not take that first step into the smoke or off the ridge. They will not go in a direction that others are not taking. The promises of the past can blind us to the new conditions of the future. We know what has worked before and wonder why it is not working now. We cannot see the ideal future and the benefits it might bring. Still others can see the ideal but wrongly think that they do not deserve the ideal, the grand, or the great.

To see differently you need to think as a wayfinder. Look at what is different in the environment; the changes may be obvious or subtle. Look at changes in relationships; the changes may be obvious or subtle. Then think about what you are seeing and how you are seeing it. Be reflexive.

In social science, seeing what you want to see is called conformational bias. The research journals are full of studies where someone names something he sees, creates a measure, and then declares a truth. The belief that something exists creates the reality of its existence. The stock markets are full of investors who, because they are investing in something, create the predicted growth. But it is not always real. Wayfinders know the difference between reality and belief.

In 1927, a scientist named Werner Heisenberg proposed a principle that says it is "impossible to simultaneously measure the present position while 'determining' the future momentum of an electron or any other particle with an arbitrary degree of accuracy and certainty. (Heisenberg, 1927) In other words, when you observe something, you change it. Heisenberg understood even in science that there is a relationship between the observer and the material world. We cannot separate ourselves from the environment that we are observing, and when we change the way we observe, we change the thing we observe. As humans, we can see, but we can also see how we are seeing. While our thinking rarely changes the environment, our environment should be able to change our thinking and lead us to a new series of productive actions. It did for Kenny Blake in a burning coalmine, and it did for me. It sometimes takes time to figure out how new thinking leads to right action.

Chapter 6:

⤙⤙❧⤚⤚

See How Others See You

I t was a honeymoon of sorts for Sue and Ray Baird. In the six months since the wedding, they had spent most of their time mending fences in the families. "It's too soon," the children would argue, "It was too soon after the deaths of their spouses."

Sue and Ray met when they were lost. Both had been married for many years. Both had happy and solid families. Both raised children with other partners. Both stayed with their partners through the diagnosis, the battle, and the loss. Cancer was their common enemy.

Instead of being paralyzed and lonely, they found a second love with a common experience. When I met the couple, both in their late sixties, in their Green Castle, Pennsylvania home. They sat close to each other and held hands. Each filled a void in the other. Each was deeply appreciated by the other. Both wanted to tell their story with the other as hero.

Sue had been a lifelong journalist working for a local newspaper. She had started as a reporter and then, later in her persistent career, became the editor of the paper. Along the way, she learned photography, typesetting, and persistence. Her former trade led her to document everything.

Ray was a driver—not a bus driver, but a coach driver. He drove the big tourist buses to Civil War battlefields, to nearby Washington, DC, to anyplace his company sent him. As a coach driver, he still had a bit of wanderlust. The highway was his second home. Sue and Ray first met in the doctor's office while their spouses were undergoing chemotherapy. Neither dreamed that they would find love again with each other a few years later. Both believe it was an act of God that brought them together, even though Ray said after sixty-eight years he was just learning how to pray.

Greencastle is about as different from northern Arizona and southern Utah as you can get. Greencastle is different shades of green everywhere; the country around Page, Arizona, is varying shades of brown. Greencastle is humid with regular waterings of rain. Page is dry and gets few rainstorms annually, usually in the form of targeted thunderstorms that bring flash floods down the washes.

In June 2008, Ray and Sue flew into Phoenix, Arizona, on their first real trip together. At one point in their lives, they had planned to take these kinds of trips with their life partners. But having been lost in grief and found in the hope of a new love, they took this adventure together.

Living on a limited budget, they rented a small car that would get good gas mileage. They bought some cola, a few bottles of water, and some snack food for the road and then headed north. The first part of the drive rises out of the Phoenix valley and into the pines of northern Arizona. At first Ray took the wheel. He was the professional driver. Sue documented everything. She took pictures and wrote in her journal.

In Flagstaff they stopped and ate lunch in a diner and then headed in to see the Grand Canyon, but it was too touristy for their liking. Perhaps the lesser-known national parks of southern Utah would be just as spectacular but less crowded and more unique. In secret, Sue wanted this trip to break the ice with her new husband. He was not as talkative as she had hoped. She wanted to get to know him better.

After seeing the Grand Canyon, they drove the long and flat road across the Navajo Indian Reservation, stopping along the way to explore the makeshift stands where real Indians sell to tourists jewelry strung of beads made in China and purchased on the internet. The few remaining real Native American artisans sell their wares to dealers for hundreds or thousands of dollars.

They spent the first night in Page, overlooking Lake Powell. Page is a multilayered town on the edge of the Navajo Nation. Its year-round economy is fueled by the nearby power plant, but the economy surges in the summer months when hoards of mariners come to the inland sea. Lake Powell is shared by Utah and Arizona, which leads to claims that these states have more shoreline than California. The blue waters follow what was once Glenn Canyon up the vast Colorado River 150 miles. To the northeast are Canyonlands and Arches national parks. To the west are Bryce and Zion national parks. Sue, who was the trip planner, had picked Capitol Reef National Park as the first stop. According to her Google map, Capitol Reef was almost due north. A road skirting the lake would lead them to Hanksville and into the park.

So armed with a set of computer-generated instructions and a printed-out map, Sue and Ray left their motel early in the morning and set out for their planned adventure. But the adventure that they had was nothing like what they expected.

After crossing the Glenn Canyon Dam and stopping for pictures, they followed the paved highway for a few miles and then turned right onto a dirt road. In their rearview mirror, they could see Page and the houses and developments that border the lake. It was a civil part of civilization. But in front of them, there were dry and arid peaks, dotted with brown and dried trees. No houses, roads, or developments were visible.

But no worries—the map was clear, with distances printed for each turn. It would be just over a hundred miles of dirt roads. As they headed into the desert wilderness, they passed a road grader working to cut out some of the bumps. The driver offered a friendly wave that helped erase any doubt that they were headed in the right direction. In her journal, Sue wrote, "The road climbed higher and higher up a steep red mountain. By the time we got to the top we were pretty unnerved. That's about when the GPS said 'for a better route…' Thanks for nothing.

"We got to the point where we were supposed to turn left, but a sign said the road was washed out. The GPS offered an alternate route. It was a longer route, but the GPS said we could get there. At that point we made what turned out to be a near-fatal mistake; we decided not to turn back, remembering the huge red mountain we had already crossed with such difficulty."

But soon they were on a steep road going up a hill that their small car strained to climb. Ray would have slipped the clutch if he had been in a coach and had a manual transmission. This automatic transmission lost too much power for his liking. They rounded a corner and found still another hill. It was wide enough for Ray to pick his route around the rocks that would likely damage the underside of this delicate rental. He was reluctant to tell Sue that he had his doubts, but she spoke first. "Maybe this is not such a good idea," she said.

Ray thought about turning around, but the road was too narrow, with a steep drop on the right side. Then the car's undercarriage hit something hard, and the engine stopped. Ray pulled the emergency brake, put the car in park, and jumped out, only to see oil leaking onto a big rock under the car's engine. The oil pan had been ruptured. Ray jumped into action. He pulled the jack out of the trunk and placed it under the high-centered car. Jacking the car up, he placed rocks under the wheels. It took four hours to coax the car off the rock and back onto the road. Slowly, they backed down the hill and turned around. "We both thanked God for our freedom," she wrote. "But it was short lived."

Starting the engine, Ray began a race. An engine without oil was not long for the road. Perhaps they could get back to the road grader or another car would come along. So far, they had seen no one. But their hope was that they could soon find someone.

The car took them about four miles, back to the wash but not up the other side. "It just stopped," Sue said. "We knew that it was dead."

Silence.

When the engine stopped, Ray cranked it a few times just to see if they could nurse another mile or two out of the rig, but his experience as a professional driver told him that this car was dead. At first, he worried about the cost of a new engine. Then he thought about the insurance deductible. Sue worried that Ray was too stressed. Neither of them worried about their predicament. They just picked up the cell phone and tried a call. Nothing—out of range.

Ray said, "At first we thought someone would be along anytime. Surely there were others going to Capitol Reef this same way. If not other tourists, the road grader would be along in a while. Clearly they were maintaining the road." In the first hour, they walked around, drank some water, and kept out of the heat. It was 80, maybe 90 degrees, but it was a dry heat that was washed away by the soda in their trunk.

Nothing is more silent than the desert. There are no trees to blow in the wind, no running water, and no noise broken by technology. In the silence of this dry riverbed, Sue found a rock a few yards from the car and began writing. It was what she always did.

"We spent the night in the car. Night comes early in the desert. The sun began to set at seven and we both managed to sleep. We awoke at 4 a.m. when the sun came up and decided to walk to Recreation Road 230, which the GPS said is 1.6 miles down the road. We walked for an hour and saw no road, so we decided to return to the car where there was food and shelter," Sue said.

In all, they had eight cans of soda, three apples, three snack bars, some pretzels, six packs of string cheese, and some crackers. After a few hours and some talk, the couple decided that they would soon be found. They told each other that when they did not check into the hotel, the clerk would call the sheriff. When they did not call the kids, the kids would call the sheriff. When the road grader driver came by again, he would stop. In the river wash, there were signs of recent cattle herding. Surely a rancher would be along soon. As the shadows got longer and the day began to die, Sue and Ray prayed together and then tried to sleep when it was dark. "We decided our best strategy was to wait to be rescued."

In the dark, the silence was deafening. She said, "I heard jets in the sky but far off. No singing morning birds that grace the wetter climates. Just an occasional caw from a crow." *They must be out in force by now*, Sue thought. She had covered many police investigations and searches. As a reporter, she had come to respect the long hours and hard work of law enforcement agencies. *They will be here soon, and we will be embarrassed.* In her mind, she rehearsed what she would say to the officer and her daughter when she was found.

In the heat of the afternoon of the second day, they began to realize that their ordeal might just be beginning. They began to ration their water and soda. That night they dined on two crackers each. "It was a good meal with a kind man," Sue said. In the cool of the evening, they began to talk. "It was the first time we realized that we might not get out of this," Sue said.

"That night we talked about everything," she said. "About our lives, our families, our hopes for the future, and our faith." They huddled together in the coolness, catching moments of sleep and listening for a rescue that did not come. At each point, Sue continued to write in her journal, reflecting deeply.

"I am usually an optimist, but I don't feel very optimistic right now. I don't want to die this way in this place. Please, God, help us find our way out of this wilderness. We need an angel of mercy."

And so passed days three and four. A couple of times they walked up the road, hoping to see a road crew or get a cell signal. Meals included a couple of crackers and some sips of soda. As they struggled, Sue's admiration for Ray began to grow. His kindness, his sensitivity, his willingness to listen, and his desire to live spurred her will to survive. In her journal she wrote, "This experience has taught me that one never knows when the end will come. I feel blessed to have been given the chance to make it right with God. I need to go off by myself tomorrow morning when it is cool and have a heart-to-heart with my creator."

In addition to the soul-searching, there were other difficult admissions. They had to admit that the hotel clerk had not called the sheriff when they did not show up. They had to admit that their children were not worried when they did not call. They had to admit that no one knew what route they had taken. They also had to admit that a plane or helicopter would have to be right on top of them before they would be seen in the wash. With those admissions, it was time to agree that they needed to take action on their own. "We realized this might be yet another mistake on our parts, but it's either stay here and die or die trying to help ourselves."

The afternoon of the fifth day was spent writing letters and amending their wills. They wrote to each person in their lives whom they loved, knowing that eventually the car would be found. Sue placed the treasured documents along with a description of their direction of travel in plain sight on the seat of the car.

At three thirty in the morning on the sixth day, they took the last can of soda from the trunk, ate the last few crackers, and headed down the wash in the direction that the cow tracks led. Ray said, "We were pretty weak, and we didn't think we would get far, but we figured it was Saturday, and if anyone was out, it would be on the weekend."

At this point, weakened with hunger, bleached by the sun, and tired from a lack of sleep, their physical condition might be seen as their greatest vulnerability. But it was not. Behind them like a shadow was fear. It followed them everywhere. It threatened to overtake them, to cause them to panic. But Sue and Ray had a shield against that fear. It was a shield built from the fibers of their love for each other. Instead of fear, they focused on faith and on helping each other take the next step and the next and the next.

The going was slow. Their weak feet pushed deep into the sandy wash. It was like walking on the beach. They put in lots of effort for little distance. When the wash opened up, they found a desert flat and saw a dirt road in the distance. They would head toward the road, hoping it was not like other roads they had been on in this vast and empty place. As the sun rose, the heat slowed their progress. Sue worried that Ray would have a heart attack. Ray worried that he might lose his second love. "We will stay together," they decided.

By two o'clock that afternoon, they were too exhausted to move, and the heat was draining their bodies of liquid. A black umbrella taken from the car provided the only shelter from the sun. The dust and the dirt did not matter anymore. They were too tired to worry about that, too tired for even another step. Ray fell fast asleep.

Then Sue heard it first. An engine. It was just another plane. No. A Jeep maybe? No. Aha, a motorcycle. Before she could focus, the cycle had passed through the wash and out of sight. Sue collapsed in disappointment. The shadow of fear had caught her. The hope of rescue was fleeting and gone. Ray shouted, determined to make something happen. They listened, but the rider was out of sight, and the sweet sound of the engine was no more.

But then it came again, this time louder. The pop and sputter sound of the two-stroke engine, annoying in the neighborhood, sounded like angels singing. Within five minutes, another motorcycle came over the hill, and this time the rider stopped. At that point, it was hard to tell who was more surprised—the old couple on their sixth day of desert survival or the rider, seeing an old couple with a black umbrella and a few cans of soda sitting in a desert nowhere.

"We learned that they had seen no one riding in the desert that day. One of them carried our belongings, and the other carried Ray, and the third said, 'Hop on, Mama.' They took us to a creek called Last Chance Creek and told us to wait there in the shade while they went for rescue." Last Chance Creek was their first chance to drink without rationing, wash without worrying, and cool off—the cool waters on their hot feet.

The rescue riders headed over the horizon, and there was silence again, but this time the emptiness of the desert was filled with hope. Within a few hours, a helicopter was dispatched, and the two were receiving medical care in the hospital in Page, Arizona.

Last Chance Network

Sue and Ray learned about their own endurance in the desert. They learned about their deep feelings for each other. They learned to solve problems together, and they learned about their social network. The advent of Facebook, MySpace, LinkedIn, and other social network sites allows us to post what we want others to see. But often, social networks give us a false sense of what is really needed from our social network. If we need clever reactions to pictures, a happy birthday or anniversary salutation, or a taunt about a favorite sports team, mediated social networks can help.

But most of us need more. We may need to provide the instrumental support of finding a job, the emotional support when we lose a loved one, or the functional support to fix a computer. These do not come through a computer screen. They can only be done in person.

The Chinese call the social network required for surviving in times of scarcity *guanxi*. You have a special obligation to people within your *guanxi*. If someone needs a job, you help him find it. If someone needs money, you loan it. If someone needs shelter, you give it. The *guanxi* ethic arose in a society where the emperor and other public officials could take your property or even enslave your family at a moment's notice. *Guanxi* identified those who would protect you if you protected them.

Knowing who is in our *guanxi* is critical to being found. It tells us who will protect us unconditionally. It also tells us who will give us honest and direct feedback. Few people will post an honest reaction to our performance, identity, or experience in a public space like a social network site. Those kinds of intimate communications are generally reserved for private conversations, but they are rare and precious gifts.

The Marine's Marine

Frank was a Marine's Marine. (I have changed his name and changed a few details at his request.) Marines are tough, but Frank was among the toughest. As a high school football linebacker, he was called The Terminator because of the number of opponents he either took out of the game or who asked to be taken out of the game because of his tough play. In college he briefly obtained a wrestling scholarship at a top school, but rumors that the program would be cut persisted, and Frank was restless in the classroom. So he joined the Marines.

In boot camp, he learned that he could lead. Already in great shape, he often carried the packs of others and encouraged them to finish. He was limber, fast, strong, and smart. He could shoot, throw, and run. He seemed up to every task they put in front of him. In an environment designed to stress, he excelled. One day the sergeant called him a Marine's Marine. The description stuck. From that day forward, he wanted to be the best Marine. His goal was to return to boot camp some day as an instructor. "Boot camp was hell for most of the guys, but it was almost fun for me. The drill instructors would hold me up as the example all the time, and that made me feel pretty good."

Upon graduation, Frank had some choices, and he chose a unit most likely to be deployed into combat. Frank liked the structure of military life with the defined status or rank of members, the regularity of schedules, and the learning challenges. He also loved the brotherhood he found with his fellow Marines. After a year of additional training, he was made corporal, and within a few years, he found himself in the first wave of troops invading Iraq.

"We hit the desert and moved, taking very little fire once we crossed the border. Even when our Humvee took some incoming from tanks, our team performed flawlessly. We took cover, called in air support, and pushed around the threat. But most of the time the fear of the Marines seemed to push the Iraqi Defense Forces right out of the way. Most of them wanted to surrender." As the tip of the spear, Frank's unit sprinted across the desert toward the metropolitan home of Saddam Hussein. It took about three days to get to Baghdad, but that was mostly because they had to stop and wait for the supply support.

On the outskirts of Baghdad, the Marines waited, playing touch football in the desert and catching up on much-needed sleep in their foxholes. As they waited, they took their first and only casualty. A mortar company stationed in the rear fired an errant shell that landed in the foxhole next to Frank's. A nineteen-year-old private just out of boot camp was killed in his sleep by what is called "friendly fire." His body was scattered across the desert, with several pieces landing on Frank while he slept.

"We did what Marines do. We sucked it up and moved on. Within a few days, we were busy restoring order in Baghdad. We hung out for a while in the famous palace that belonged to Saddam."

Frank was in Iraq for six more months. While he was in several firefights, he never knowingly killed anyone or saw any other casualties. Still, it bothered him that this Marine, this hardly-a-man from some little Midwestern town, this guy who no one really knew, had been killed not by the enemy but by another Marine. "We knew how to deal with the enemy," he told me. "We just did not know how to deal with this."

In Kuwait his unit waited for three weeks before they could fly home. They spent much of that time doing "chores" for the camp and playing touch football. It still felt like they were in a war zone, and "you never really sleep in a war zone," according to Frank. "You doze, with one eye open and senses still engaged so that at the first sound of gunfire you are ready to hit back."

"I got on the plane and settled in and went to sleep for sixteen hours. It was the first time in six months that I did not have to sleep with one eye open. It was sweet."

Frank was given an extended leave when he arrived in the United States, and he returned to be with his parents. It was the first time in three and a half years that he had lived with them, in his old room, with his high school sports trophies on the shelves, with the lawn mowers going on Saturday morning, and with the sweet smell of home cooking floating down the hall.

Frank's younger brother wanted to know everything, and Frank told him about it all—the firefights, the palace, the kids in the street who became your friends. He told it all, except about the casualty. But after the stories were told and the hero status diminished, Frank found himself spending more and more time in his room. He liked the familiarity and the safety of his room. He began sleeping longer hours and staying close to home. Soon he was literally staring at the walls for much of the day. He didn't know what he wanted; he didn't know what to do. And soon sleep was hard to come by. His mind would wander back to Iraq, back to Baghdad, back to the foxhole, back to the night when the single mortar shell took his fellow Marine in the foxhole just a few feet away.

When friends and family would reach out, Frank would erupt. He did not want to be a charity project. Finally, one night after his mother asked how she could help, Frank heard himself yelling. "You don't know what it is like! You don't understand. How could you help?"

In a few weeks, it was time for Frank to report for duty again. It took every ounce of courage, every muscle he had, to drag himself to the airport. "It was much harder to return to duty than it was to go into combat in the first place. I don't know why I was so scared."

Frank's behaviors after his return to duty set off a series of red flags in the Marine Corps. At first, he wanted to return to combat as soon as possible. Then he wanted a desk job. Finally, he did not want to be a Marine at all. Within a year, he had been discharged and was at home again in his room, with his family watching his anger and reclusion grow.

His mother described the fights and the yelling. "They were mostly one way. We would ask how we could help. He would yell."

Frank knew he was lost, but he seemed to be able to do nothing about it. "I was in a bad way with no way out. The only ambition I had was dead. I had lost my desire and my hopes and my dreams. I didn't have anything to do. I spent too much time in my room, alone, going over the dark things in my mind."

Three Visitors

Frank tried a job, and he tried college, but his first attempts were weak at best. He would go, give it a great effort for a day, return the second day with a bad attitude, and then walk away from the opportunity. For a while, friends came around, and a few times Frank went out with them; most came to see Frank as a charity case, hard to be around, and difficult to talk to. He was mercurial, rude, and sometimes downright angry.

His parents feared the isolation. Any direct suggestion they made to Frank just set him off. They called a Veterans Administration counselor and tried to get help, but Frank would not go. They talked to friends, family, other vets, and clergy. No one seemed to get through. Finally, it was Frank's mother who had the idea.

"Frank's old football coach was now an assistant coach at a small junior college that had a new football program. Even though Frank had not played in four years, he was still in pretty good shape. I called Coach and asked him if he might consider Frank for the team. He did one better. He came over to the house, met with Frank for two hours, then left. A few minutes later Frank came out of his room and said, 'I think I'm going to play football.' I cried."

Frank began workouts, and quickly his maturity and toughness gave him an advantage over the mostly younger players, though he had lost some speed. It was a start-up team, not expected to win many games, and no other schools had recruited most of the players. Frank was offered a scholarship and began taking classes. Games began, and because the college had a new program and because most students worked, the crowds were small, smaller than high school. But it did not matter to Frank. His parents, his brother, and even a few new friends came to the games.

"It was great to be out there again. We were a pretty lousy team. We won only two games that year, and those were flukes. We lost a couple of games by fifty points. Those were not flukes. We were pretty bad, but we loved playing the game."

In the final home game of the season, Frank glanced up into the stands to see his parents. A young woman was sitting next to his mother, talking with her as if they were old friends. It took a while, but he recognized her as someone he had gone out with briefly in high school. Next to her was a little girl who looked like she was two or three years old. The girl was playing with a doll and not paying attention to the game, but then neither was Frank. The whole sight seemed surreal to him. There was his old friend Lisa with his mom watching him from the stands. Initially, he thought she might be babysitting a niece or the child of a friend and hoped that they could get together.

"The moment I saw her, I felt like I turned a corner. I realized I was getting better. Coach called. I was on the field, and I blew the next play because I was thinking about how to ask Lisa out. After the game, there she was with Mom and Dad. But I was focused on her. After a few moments, I said I needed to hit the showers but asked if we could get together sometime. She said, 'Yeah, but I'll need to get a babysitter for my daughter.'"

Lisa had been a serious student in high school. She had gone off to college, quickly married, had a child, graduated, and divorced. Her ex-husband put the two in his rearview mirror and never looked back. Frank was the first real date she'd gone on since her divorce. They went out a few nights later, and Frank's mom was the babysitter. Later Frank found out that his mother had run into Lisa at the grocery store and invited her to the game. He knew he was getting better, because he did not erupt and accuse his mother of meddling or "trying to manage his life."

Soon they were spending most of their time together. Lisa encouraged Frank to stay up on his schoolwork, and Coach kept the pressure on to keep working out. There was real progress, but not complete progress. "He was sort of hard to be with," Lisa told me. "He would just clam up and not say anything. Other times, he would just get quiet and stay away."

Many nights Frank would wake up after a nightmare. He would push all the covers off the bed and shake the pillows, afraid that body parts were in his bed. There was no rational override. He would have to clear the bed. He also still had anger problems that cost him a suspension from a game and almost cost him a scholarship for the second year. He didn't want to lose the team. It felt like the Marines again. They had even won a few games.

One night, after a dinner with Lisa, Frank began talking about his time in Iraq and told her what he had told only a handful of people. He told her about the "friendly fire shell and the death of the young Marine. I did not even really know him. He was a young guy and was fresh out of boot camp. Then Lisa said something that stunned me. 'Maybe it would help to go see his folks,' she said. At that point, I realized that I had been making this whole thing about myself, saying 'it could have been me' or feeling guilty for not being his friend. She helped me realize that his parents were hurting like hell."

A few weeks later, Frank boarded a plane for Iowa, rented a car, and visited the parents of the fallen Marine. It had been more than two years since his comrade's death, but his parents were still grieving. Together they talked, they cried, they looked at pictures. When Frank got up to leave, the father of the fallen Marine asked to take his photograph.

"Why?" said Frank, doubting he would ever see these people again.

"To put it with the others," he said.

"What others?"

"The thirteen other Marines who have come by since our boy fell."

Frank was stunned.

"This one fired the shell."

The Light of the Rising Sun

On their fifth day, as the eastern sky went from grey to pink, Sue and Ray Baird abandoned their assumptions about being rescued by a concerned and caring network. It was their first step toward rescue. "We needed to realize that others were not going to come and get us out of this mess. It was up to us," said Sue. It was hard and it was risky, but it was a decision that saved them.

But more important than what others think is what they will do. What kinds of support will they provide? They come with valuable offerings like information and mindful listening—information to help make a clear decision, listening to help us know what we know, emotional support to defuse fears, instrumental support to solve a problem, network support to connect us with needed expertise. Support is different from love. Support is an action—and it produces a result.

Frank, in his darkest times, had support. His relentless parents brought new light back into his life slowly, creating new relationships and repairing old ones. Like the gradually rising sun, Frank began to see the importance of new people in his life who led to school, work opportunity, and family. But most of all, it allowed him to shift his role away from being a victim—and away from the darkness of his room.

I last saw Frank in the graduation procession. He had completed a four-year degree in accounting. He told me about his three visitors that turned his life around—a coach, a woman, and a family in Iowa. His wife, Lisa, and her daughter, whom he was helping to raise, were in the audience with his parents. As we were talking, the little girl ran down the steps and jumped into his arms. "And then there is this one," he said.

Lost people becoming found use their social network like a mirror. Sometimes mirrors distort and bend the light, but most of the time they give a fairly accurate picture of who you are. Sometimes the only way you can know who you are is by hearing what others say about you.

The last time I spoke with Sue and Ray Baird they were living in Florida and taking frequent trips to various parts of the United States to visit family. Both say they are grateful to God for their time in the southern Utah desert. "We learned a lot about ourselves, our faith, and our family," said Sue.

Chapter 7:

You Are Never Lost Alone

"I should tell you how we ended up here in the mud, in the middle of nowhere. We were just so excited about seeing the country, you know, we had never gone that route before," she said. "Just looking forward to a beautiful sunny day and looking forward to our destination too." Rita Chretien wrote in her diary for each of the forty-nine days she spent marooned in Nevada's Humboldt National Forest in a van, stuck in the mud.

In March 2011, Al and Rita left their small town in British Columbia to drive to a contractors' convention in Las Vegas. She was looking forward to seeing some of the most remote areas in the continental United States, but she did not expect to be in a place where the only signs of civilization on the vast horizon are dirt roads. Rita was not even sure how they got there. They had gassed up in Boise, Idaho, and she had fallen asleep. There were times in her slumber that she was aware that the road had become rough. What woke her was the sound of the spinning wheels. They were stuck in the mud and had slid off a dirt road.

The Humboldt National Forest is a maze of logging roads and makeshift hunting roads ninety miles north of Elko, Nevada. Some parts of the area are open grass; other parts are dense forest. The whole area of northern Nevada is one of the most sparsely populated areas in one of the least densely populated states in the United States. There are a few small towns, a few mines, a few ranches, and a few nomadic people.

Rita wrote, "It was very country road for many kilometers then the road got more like back-road trail. The GPS still indicated all the turns, so we kept on. We soon started thinking this doesn't look good ... but we followed GPS directions, and we got stuck in the mud around 10:00 p.m. It turned out to be a logging road. Wow, we felt dumb and discouraged."

Of course, they expected a car to come along soon. If they had gotten there, someone else would. They waited. The conversation was optimistic, but Al started to stress. She suggested, "'Look, it's very late, and we're tired. Let's just sleep in the van, and in the morning we'll know what to do.'" We just couldn't believe what had happened. Al cried, and I cried. And we prayed unto the Lord, 'What do we do now?'"

On the second day, she said, "We knew in the morning we were in trouble. We climbed the hill and attempted to call 911. We got through and gave a few GPS positions, but we got cut off ... out of gas almost, we had prayed earnestly for help to come. We said, 'Please Lord.'"

Al and Rita began walking and again reached for their GPS. After seven and a half kilometers of walking, Rita's injured knee began hurting. They turned back. If they had gone the opposite direction of where the GPS led them, they would have arrived at a ranch, eight miles away from their van.

"We maybe were a little bit in a panic. We were frustrated and tried different positions on the GPS. Nothing made sense.

We couldn't see any sign of civilization anywhere—for miles," Rita said. "We realized the GPS wasn't working, and we were very mixed up. We felt dumb and discouraged. So thank the Lord we packed blankets and snacks."

Rita wrote that they were well aware of how desperate their situation was. So on day three, March 21, 2011, Al decided he would try to walk toward Mountain City. Guided by a careful plan made using the GPS, Al wrote down which direction he would go at each intersection. He made a copy and left the directions with Rita who would wait in the van.

"[I thought] so here we are, stuck and probably nobody knows, except God."

"And we prayed and we cried, and he went," she said. "I tried to compose myself so he would be able to go. If I had been very emotional, he never would have gone. So I tried to be strong for him, so he could go," she wrote. Rita was left alone, with her diary and her increasing loneliness. As Al walked off, he desperately wanted to be a hero. She took one last photo. As he walked up the road and rounded the bend, he turned for one last wave and blew Rita a kiss.

The Neighbor: Hanna's Search

During those long days when Rita sat in a van writing in her diary, her network was at work. Spurred by a caring friend and a conscientious police office, by a minister and family members, her network pushed out to bring her home. What drives big, happy golden retrievers to search all day in desert heat or mountain snow to find a victim? The "treat" or "play reward" is only how you get them started—it is what you do as a dog handler to show appreciation. But the primary reason dogs push themselves hard and then harder, beyond play and master loyalty, is pack loyalty.

Dogs are pack animals. They prefer, like their ancestors the wolf, to live in families that we call packs. Domesticated dogs have shifted their loyalty from the dog pack to the human pack. You see misguided pack behavior when a stranger approaches and your dog growls. The animal is not thinking it is in danger. It is thinking the pack, and that means you, is threatened by the stranger.

The positive side of pack behavior for dogs is their ability to search until the lost pack member is found. When you give a dog a search command, you are essentially telling the dog that the pack is not complete and that they need to complete it. The dog then goes in search of the missing family member whom it may never have met. When the dog is searching, it is all business. The dog focuses, even obsesses, on finding a scent that will lead it to the right source. When the search dog finds a lost subject, its tail goes up, its body straightens, it gets more energy even if it is tired, and it returns to the Alpha (the handler) with great enthusiasm hoping for recognition of the job well done.

Hanna Hyland has the same instincts. She takes being a neighbor seriously. It is a theological, spiritual, and practical responsibility that doesn't have much to do with whom you live next door to. If you are in Hanna's social network, then she believes that she is responsible for your well-being. So to Hanna, a neighbor is a person for whom she feels an abiding responsibility based on sisterly love. Hanna was Rita's neighbor by this definition.

When Rita and Al did not return from their trip to Las Vegas, Hanna noticed. She began communicating with Rita's children, and together they called authorities. "Then we called the hotel in Las Vegas where they were supposed to be staying," Hanna said. "Our hearts sunk when we found out that they had never checked into their room."

Supported by her husband, Ken; Rita and Al's three children; and the Royal Canadian Mounted Police (RCMP), Hanna and the authorities began their search. The last known whereabouts for Rita and Ken was more than a week ago in a small town in Oregon where they had bought gas. The purchase was unremarkable. They just bought gas and a few snack items.

The RCMP, in cooperation with US law enforcement agencies, did what they could, but the search area and the possibilities seemed unlimited. Was it a crime? A planned disappearance? A case of irresponsibility? A full tank of gas meant the couple in the van could be in Oregon, Idaho, Nevada, Utah, or even California or Wyoming. They could also have backtracked into Washington. With hundreds of missing people in the United States, law enforcement agencies are reluctant to put too many resources into a case like this one that has no starting point, no actual crime, and no agreed upon scenario. But that did not stop Hanna. She made the search a full-time job.

She began online and on the phone contacting police agencies in each county in Oregon, Idaho, and Nevada. She printed a flyer and a description of the van. Then she called police agencies to remind them to remind their officers to be on the lookout.

After a few days, she started another strategy. Using a network of church affiliations, she sent emails with flyers to ministers, requesting that they ask their congregations to look for Rita and Al. She also asked those who owned businesses in the high-probability area to put up posters and flyers. Hundreds of people responded with more than prayers. They also responded with action that brought this case to the interest of more and more people. But despite the interest, there were just no clues to where Rita and Al could be. No one expected that they were off the road in one of the most remote places in the continental United States.

The Messenger

It had been four days since they had become stuck in the mud, and Rita had been alone for two of those days. The days were short and cold, with only a little sunlight leaking into the van. The nights were long and dark and colder. The gas tank was now empty and the battery was dead. Al had taken half of the water and one of the two bags of trail mix; he left her with a bag of trail mix, some hard candy, and fish oil vitamins. As Rita stared into this hopeless situation, fear stalked her every move.

But then a friend came. "I was sitting in the van when this little bird came to the windshield singing and chirping. He was just a little grey thing, a sparrow, perhaps." From then on, she would see the bird frequently. "Every time I felt so alone, this bird would be there singing for me, and so I thought of singing back. I sang whatever I could remember, but mostly church songs," she said.

So Rita settled in, making the van as comfortable as possible without Al. At first, she thought it might take a day or two. She wondered where Al was. Had he passed this point or that? Was he warm? The first night there was a blizzard, according to sheriff deputies, but Rita did not see it or remember it. On day two, she began rationing her trail mix and assessing her food situation. Worried about dehydration, she took water off the windshield and from a nearby stream. "The water was dirty, but it tasted good," she wrote in her diary. "It tasted good. Tasted sweet, even though it was dirty."

"I had a little Rubbermaid container, and I'd have a sponge bath inside. And I didn't want anyone to find me real dirty and stinky; that wouldn't do," she said.

At night, she would ask herself which "hotel" she would stay in. Sometimes she would curl up on the passenger seat of the van; other times she would stretch out in the passenger seat or driver's seat. She had a blanket that was always kept in the van and a couple of warm baby blankets that she had thrown in at the last minutes despite Al's objection. "Never hurts to have more than you need." Without them, she would have faced impossible cold.

The space where Rita was surviving was barren, with just a few bushes and grass. A hundred yards away, near the stream, was some growth. She built a small fire pit near the van and gathered what fuel she could. With some scraps of paper, she was able to use a magnifying glass to create a flame, but the fuel was always too wet and did not want to burn. So most days were spent reading and in the sun—the warm sun—whenever it was shining.

"I went up to a rock overlooking the van where I could marvel at God's creations, and I sat in the sun. Often my little bird friend would follow," she said. Rita thought about trying to walk out, but in the evening she would see deer and coyotes and one morning found what were likely cougar footprints around the van. Fear of being attacked limited her willingness to be adventuresome.

"By the second week, I assumed something bad had happened," she said. "I could not think that Al was okay on his own in this wilderness. I kept thinking of the kiss that he blew me as he passed out of sight and the feeling that I had that that would be the last time I would see him."

"There were times I didn't know what to do. I would just say, 'What do I do now Lord? Show me what to do,' especially in the mornings when I really didn't want to go out of the van for fear of wild beasts," she said. "I would just say, 'Lord, help me. I know I need to get fresh air. I can't stay in the van.' I would go out for fifteen-minute walks every day.… I really don't like being alone, even in a crowd.… Now, I was very alone. The only way I could get through it was by praying and trusting the Lord to be with me and trust that somehow He would get me through this every day. It helped that fear fade. Every day the fear was less. I would look forward every day to talking with God every day when I woke up. I would say, 'Good morning, Lord. Here I am.' I learned that maybe His time is not my time."

Rita filled the time by taking pictures of things she saw hope in. She looked at a field where she would imagine a rescue helicopter landing. "I ate my candy and fish oil tablets. I tasted many things, and nothing sat right. I decided to just stick to my candy and my fish oil. I started to pretend I had things like macaroni and a hot dog. I would hold my hands out and pretend the food was there. And I would ask the Lord to bless it and give me the nutrition I would have gotten if I ate it. Then the hunger went away—for that meal anyway."

"There were a few times I broke down and really bawled my eyes out for a few hours. Other than that, I focused on what I needed to do. I read my books and just decided to hang in there."

When the books were read, she began writing in her diary about her life, her faith, and her predicament. "I wanted my kids to know about what took us to that point, and I wanted to know myself what I was learning in this trial." During these long days she planned her garden; she also planned Al's memorial service complete with the menu for the memorial dinner. But after forty days in the van, living on less than two hundred calories a day, she began to wear out.

"It was at the forty-day mark when I felt weak. It was harder and harder to get down the hill to get the water." At this point, Rita began planning her own memorial service.

"On the forty-ninth day, I literally had to crawl up from the stream on my hands and knees. When I got to the van, I changed my socks, cleaned myself up, covered myself with blankets, and prepared to die."

"Now I lay me down to sleep," she sang, hoping her bird would hear her. "I pray the Lord my soul to keep."

She slept not expecting to wake.

The Hunter

On day forty-nine of Rita's ordeal, Troy Sill, his daughter Whitney, and his son-in-law Chad Herman arose early and fueled up their all-terrain vehicles. It was an annual ritual to go into the Humboldt and look for discarded elk antlers. "It's fun to get out," said Troy, "and if you find a few antlers, then you can almost pay for the gas." The real reason to go antler hunting was to be together in a beautiful remote country. "It's our backyard," said Troy, "and our playground."

After their first find, Chad and Whitney headed one direction, but Troy went another. "So we just turned around and followed Dad," Whitney said. "It was like he was on a mission."

"I knew where I wanted to go," said Troy. "But I was not sure why I wanted to go there."

As they came up over a hill, they were surprised to discover a minivan stuck in the mud and off to the side of the road. Troy just headed past. "I wondered what a bunch of hippies would be doing up this far away from anything at this time of year. Then I saw a little sign in the window that said "help.'" Troy stopped his machine, and as the others pulled up, he noticed a head moving in the van. Rita Chretien was inside.

"Thank God," said an emotional Mrs. Chretien. "I'm going to live."

Chad Herman told a local paper: "She was in pretty bad shape and couldn't stand up for more than a few seconds." Because cell phones didn't work in their remote location and Rita Chretien was too weak to ride on an ATV, they decided to head the nearest ranch eight miles away. "I went back and told Rita we were going to go for help and would be back in an hour. I also asked her if she would be okay by herself for another hour, and she said she would be fine. I told her two more times that we would be back in an hour."

Within an hour, a rescue helicopter was dispatched, and Rita was ready to go.

"When we got to the van," said Herman, "Rita was standing next to it with her purse on ready to go."

"We were blown away by the mental and physical strength Rita had to endure. She is a very strong and amazing woman. We didn't do anything, in our minds, that was heroic or any different than what anyone else would do," Herman said. "We tried to keep our names from getting out and didn't want any reward or attention from it. The sheriff finally got a hold of us, along with the reporters. The sheriff reported, "We just want everyone to know that our thoughts and prayers are with Rita and her family, and we are hoping that they are blessed with one more miracle in finding their father."

Rita's Reaction

Rita did not expect to wake up. She had not given up as much as she had become realistic about her situation. So when she heard an engine, she thought it might be the sound of death in her ears. But it was too familiar. It was too close. There were voices and moving shapes. She pulled the blankets off and stuck her head up. Her eyes met Troy's, and there was a moment of mutual surprise. "I don't think he expected to see me. I must have looked like a ghost," Rita remembered.

By now, the others had joined Troy at the van, and Rita blurted out her story.

"They could not believe that I had been there for so long. They thought I was crazy and just didn't know what I was talking about. So I grabbed my diary and shook my finger at them and said, 'Look here. I can prove that I was here." Rita said Troy and his two companions started shaking. "They were really traumatized," she said. "And they started talking about what to do."

Rita was surprised when all three rescuers promised to return in a couple of hours and headed off on their ATVs. "They left me alone again, and once they left, I just collapsed in the van. I knew that I had been saved and that I needed to find a new purpose."

Rita cleaned up the van, washed herself with her remaining water, and waited, dosing in the midday sun that somehow seemed warmer than before. Within a few hours, she heard another engine. It was the sound of a helicopter that passed ahead of three ATVs to find her. It landed on the side of the hill; in a blur, she was in the air, headed toward a hospital in Twin Falls, Idaho. The rush of adrenalin into her weakened body had caused her to fade in and out of consciousness. The hunger put her at the edge of life, and the hope of seeing her loved ones kept her there until medical care could take over.

"There I was in the hospital," she said, "with all these faces starring at me with loving looks. I thought they were angels."

Word spread quickly. Within a few hours, the Royal Canadian Mounted Police knocked on the doors of Rita's three children. For weeks, they had delivered the frustrating news of a failed search. Now they were saying, "They found your mother, and she is alive." But the second part of the sentence was the glass half empty. "We still don't know where Al is."

The Public Servant

Sometimes Sergeant David Prall felt like a frontier sheriff in the Wild West. He had to do everything in the crossroads town of Elko. Everything meant major crimes investigations, traffic stops, settling neighbor disputes, and search and rescue. Elko is a mining town, a railroad town, a ranching town, and a gambling town on I-80 halfway between Salt Lake and Reno going east to west and Boise and Las Vegas going north to south. Every day the city motels would fill with truckers and other cross-country strangers. Sometimes those strangers would bring their problems with them. They would drink too much, gamble too much, or just hit someone. For Prall, that was the hard part of the job.

He preferred helping his neighbors. His willingness to help is well known in the small town of people who struggle to make a living in a casino, restaurant, gold mine, or ranch. Prall liked law enforcement in an environment where he could count on his solid personal relationships to resolve situations before they got out of hand.

Most of Prall's neighbors had some sort of a tie to the outdoors. They hunted, prospected, or just went camping with the family. They would go to the Ruby Valley to the south or the Humboldt National Forest to the north. Both areas are premier elk hunting grounds. All-terrain vehicles, campers, and pickup trucks were prized above all other possessions, because you needed a reliable vehicle to get to the wilderness playground. Sometimes, not often, a friend or a neighbor would get into trouble in those wilderness playgrounds. They would be reported missing, or there would be an accident. Then Prall would call his posse—a group of volunteers who called themselves the Elko County Search and Rescue Team.

Prall worked carefully to select his SAR team and provide them the training they needed, even though time and money were scarce and the kinds of problems they faced varied. Most SAR teams train in specific kinds of search and rescue common to their area. If there are big rivers, they train in white-water search and rescue. Near mountains, high angle rescue. In urban cities, grid and rubble search. In rural environments, and as you can get in the United States, they see a variety of problems, but wilderness search is an essential skill. That's why Prall had an advantage. In Elko, people were raised on wilderness survival. They had all been hunting with the family, stayed out overnight around a fire, and been caught in a winter storm. Prall had a SAR team that was very heavy on practical experience.

So when the call came from dispatch that there was a man missing in the Humboldt, he was confident his team could and would find the victim and find him soon. He could trust his people. But the details were puzzling. The dispatcher said they had found a Canadian woman named Rita Chretien who had been missing for a couple of months. Prall had seen the missing persons report and had reminded other officers to keep their eyes out for the couple who had been missing from Canada. He knew they had come down from British Columbia on their way to Las Vegas and that their last stop had been in Oregon. He had looked for the couple and their missing van in Elko, and he had fielded phone calls from church members, part of Hanna Hyland's network, who pressed him to keep looking. Now the woman was in a hospital two hundred miles away in Idaho, and she said her husband was still up there.

When more details came in, Prall was stunned to learn that the woman had survived in her van for forty-nine days. Anyone with that kind of fortitude got instant admiration from those who called the Humboldt their backyard.

Prall called Idaho Falls and got more details. Rita Chretien reported that on the third day, forty-five days earlier, her husband had gone to get help. Now she was requesting that they launch an immediate search in an area still covered in snow to find Al. Rita had stayed in the van and barely survived. Prall knew that without shelter, Al would not have survived. He had been missing for six weeks in one of the most remote areas in the continental United States during the coldest time of the year. Yet here was this woman, this fragile and faithful woman, who survived. Now she was asking, pleading, that they search for Al.

To top it off, she had instructions. She had details on where to search. Before blowing Rita a last kiss good-bye, Al wrote out on a paper the route he would follow based on the GPS map. He took a copy with him, and he left a copy of the instructions with Rita—prophetic. He had planned to walk twenty-one miles to Mountain City along a specific route detailed in writing. This would be an easy search—no need to call for additional resources.

On the first day, the hasty team, the first group of searchers, followed Al's route, looking for circling birds and other signs of human remains. A fine police dog trained in cadaver search covered the high-probability areas, but there was nothing—no signs. By day two and three, volunteers from other Nevada counties and Boise, Idaho, had joined the search. Some 120 people covered the roads Al said he would follow. While Al's family and friends assumed that he could survive as Rita did, Prall knew differently. Rita had shelter, water, and some food. Al had nothing but what he had on his back. A leather jacket and a backpack with snacks and food could not sustain a person for forty-five days. There were no shelters, no houses, no busy roads along the way.

To make matters worse, Prall had checked the weather history. Al had left on a blue-sky day, clear and cool. But within twenty-four hours, the weather had turned. A major snowstorm with winds twenty to thirty miles per hour had poured out of the northeast and blanketed the hills with six inches of snow. Winds had drifted the snow three feet in some places. Prall knew how hard it was to survive in those conditions in a leather jacket. He wanted to believe Rita's hope; he wanted to reward her faith, but his experience told him something else. Besides, despite the evidence to the contrary, Prall had to check all possibilities. Was this a staged event? A crime? Intentional? He doubted it, but he needed to eliminate all possibilities.

As the search expanded, Prall faced other difficult questions. He had to ask himself: *How long? How long do we search? How many hours do we put in before we say that we can't find him? How much of our budget do we spend? How many volunteer hours do we ask for? How much risk do we expose searchers to as they weed their way through the side roads and canyons?*

At first, Prall assumed Al would have stayed on his planned route. He assumed that his body was lying in the sagebrush off a dirt road. As the days went, on other theories were explored. Perhaps he had become disoriented in the snowstorm and tacked a wrong road. Checking the road spurs and trails greatly expanded the search area but still yielded nothing. After twelve days and almost two thousand man-hours of searching, Prall made the difficult decision to suspend the search. His team was exhausted, his budget long spent, and volunteers needed to return to their jobs and families.

It is always a difficult decision to suspend a search. He had to admit temporary defeat, but the cost of certainty was too high. The cost of knowing exactly what happened to Al was more that he could bear. Prall called his boss, Rita's friend, Hannah, and Rita. These were not easy calls to make. The simple search had yielded nothing—no clues, no body, no Al. Everyone had a theory, but no one had anything that was concrete.

Later in the year, Prall would go into the area several times, exploring possible leads and theories. Haunted by the unfinished business, he called Rocky Mountain Rescue Dogs and another group of volunteers to search stretches of road that had still been covered in snow during the initial search.

The Searchers

It was a late night phone call that brought Dusty and me into this search. I had heard that Elko County was going to make one more push to try to find Al before the weather changed. He had been missing now for seven months, so we knew we were looking for remains. The family and friends in Canada had pressured governors, county commissioners, sheriffs, and deputies for one more push.

Elko County Search and Rescue were the first responders when hunters found Rita. That triggered a massive search for Al that involved five hundred searchers from four states over ten days. Aided by Al and Rita's careful rescue plan, searchers scoured along every road, campsite, and structure between the van and Mountain City. Knowing that exposure and hypothermia create disorientation, searchers continued, following all the possible routes to no avail.

Now Rocky Mountain Rescue Dogs, a few Elko County Search and Rescue volunteers, and the overworked Elko County Sheriff's Deputies gathered before sunrise for a briefing. We were to search again the areas that had been snow-covered during the original search in May. We were to cover less than 2 percent of the original search area with ten people and five dogs in a long, twelve-hour day.

The search area was about five miles from where Rita had spent seven long weeks in the van. It is mostly open country, with sage, cedar trees, and some fences. In the small valleys, there were trees near water. Still, on the open ridges, you could see for miles and miles, but aside from the dirt road, there was no sign of anything man-made.

It was a tremendous task. We assumed that Al had gone west, based on the photo Rita had taken and the plan that he had. We assumed that he had gone far. But did the blizzard drive him back toward the van? Did he continue? If he had gone as far as he and Rita did the previous day, perhaps he could see the ranch lights or a cell tower five or six miles farther down the road. The only possible clue was found in the first search. An Elko County Sheriff's Deputy found a cell phone battery by the side of the road. It was a battery made for a Canadian cell phone.

We searched all day, finding the remains of various animals and seeing hunters and wildlife. We even found bones that upon examination were animal and not human. At the end of the day, in the debriefing session, we stood in a circle and Deputy Dave Prath listened while reported and speculated.

"Maybe he headed back to the van and passed it in the dark," someone speculated. Prath would then tell us how hard they worked that scenario in the first search.

"What if he took the less direct route to Mountain City?" Prath would then explain how they worked two hundred to three hundred yards off each road for days in the first search.

It was clear that the first search had been extensive, as extensive as a small county in Nevada with 150 volunteers can afford to do, and then some. At the end of a day of searching, Prath said, "We are looking for a needle in a haystack, and we don't know where the haystack is."

Looking for the Haystack

On the first brisk October morning that I searched, I thought we could make a difference, but by the end of the day, I realized that our team had covered just a small portion of the vast search area. I found bone fragments that turned out to be from animals. Dusty worked hard for eight hours, but eventually, he wore himself out following nothing. Al was not there, in my search area or in any others that were assigned to my colleagues.

The hope was that in the fall, when the hills filled with hunters, that someone would see something. But the first snowfall covered the ground and dashed those hopes, and when winter hit, the search was moved to a low priority. "When we finally find something," Prall said, ever hopeful, "we are just going to be surprised, because we had completely covered any of the obvious possibilities."

In April 2012, Hanna Hyland helped Rita organize a memorial service for Al in their hometown. It had been more than a year since she had seen him walk around the corner of the road and into the wilderness, blowing kisses. *Dear Al. Brave Al.* She often though about his last moments and prayed his remains would be undisturbed by wild animals.

The memorial service helped with some closure, but still, she wondered. How far did he make it? Did he find a cabin or cave and survive? Is he wandering without memory somewhere? Wondering took so much effort. After a few months, she began to plan a trip to return to her campsite where the van had been stuck. She would take the van that had been her shelter and had been restored with Hanna, and a few friends, and show them where she lived for forty-nine days. As plans came together, she contacted Troy, the man who had first found her, and he agreed to guide the group. It would be the first time they would meet since the helicopter whisked her away. She also planned a stop in Idaho Falls to meet the medical team who had helped with her recovery.

After some delays, the trip came together in October 2012. Rita and Hanna knew that I was trying to write their story, and they kindly invited me to join them. We met in a casino coffee shop and drove in two vehicles fifty miles north to Wild Horse Reservoir and then onto dirt roads to the high meadow where Rita had spent forty-nine days. Even after eighteen months, the tire marks where the van had skidded off the road were still visible, so was the fire ring where Rita had unsuccessfully tried to light a fire. She showed us the stream where she had drank muddy water and the hill where she would sit in the sun and pray for Al's return. And she looked for the bird that had been her company but would not say if she had seen it.

As we went to leave, someone suggested a prayer. We stood in a circle. Rita prayed in her quiet voice, acknowledging that she may never know what happened to Al but grateful for the years they had spent together. In reverent silence, we accepted that we would never know.

For seven weeks Rita wrestled with the fear of scarcity. Hunger followed her everywhere, like a dark shadow. She fought it valiantly, but some days, some hours, and some minutes, she was not able to fight back. On the last day, just before she was found, she said, "I didn't even have energy to pray." She did not fear death. It was the fear of being alone, the scarcity of affiliation, of love, that was most troubling. If Al was gone, what was there to live for? Thirty-four years of marriage, of companionship, of conversation, of shared life experiences, defined her. Rita is a quiet, shy, almost timid person. But she is not weak. Not by any imagination. "Even now, my faith is still keeping me going and helping me face the many challenges," she says. "I believe it's getting me through each day with a positive attitude and helping me carry on with my new responsibilities running our business."

Ten days after our return trip, hunters found a backpack by a tree on Merritt Mountain. Under the tree they found the undisturbed remains of Al Chretien.

Sergeant Prall believed that Al followed his planned route for six or seven miles. As the blizzard hit or with night coming on, he decided to take a shorter but harder route over the mountain. Just short of the summit, Al left his pack where it might be seen by a helicopter and climbed under a tree to rest. One he stopped moving, his sweat-drenched body would chill quickly. At first he would shiver, then he would be cold, and then he would sleep. He died of exposure, likely within twenty-four hours of leaving the van and well before anyone even knew he was missing.

We will never know why he left the path that he had so carefully planned and ventured into a place we did not search, but like many who came to know him by searching for him, I believe his last words were a prayer and his last thoughts were for his beloved Rita.

Use the QR scanner on your smart phone to watch
"The Search for Al Chretien," a three-minute video by the
author. (Also available at Lessonsoftheost.com)

Chapter 8:

Movement Creates Opportunity

The light from the full moon did not make the woods less scary for Jared. Every shadow seemed like a moving creature. Every sound sent him staring in the direction of the noise. Was it a rescuer? His fellow Boy Scouts? His mother? Or was it what he feared most, an animal that had been following his trail?

An hour before dark he had run into a mother moose with a calf, one of the most dangerous wildlife encounters possible. At first, he felt all the fear of his situation wash over him, but he quickly fought back the fear and panic and remembered not to move. He hugged a tree and let the moose pass. The incident gave him confidence, but still, here he was, half a fishing pole in hand and just the clothes on his back, lost in the woods somewhere near Daggett Lake in Utah.

The night before, he had been cold in his sleeping bag, in his tent, with fellow scouts around. Like most scouts, they had stayed up, with adult-demanded whispers becoming loud conversation, followed by a request for quiet from the scoutmaster. Once all the silliness was spent, he had drifted off to sleep, hoping for the big fish and the big adventure the next day. Now he was by himself with nothing but his fear and his fishing gear. Just after lunch Jared had walked down to the lake from the scout camp. The scoutmaster had insisted that scouts carry ten essential survival items with them at all times. He had also insisted that scouts stay with their assigned buddies. But Jared was just going to the river a few hundred feet away. The lure of fish and a chance for a little solitude canceled out the voice of the scoutmaster that would echo in his head for the next twenty-four hours.

From the stream, he could hear the camp. Boys' relentless teasing and leaders' voices rambled over the meadow. But then the stream moved faster, and the sound of moving water drowned out the voices. *No fish in this part of the stream*, Jared thought to himself. Maybe he might do better farther down the meadow. *No fish in this hole, still farther down.* It was nice to be in nature on a blue-sky sunny day. The 30-degree temperatures of the previous night were long forgotten in the warm sun. It felt good to be away from the noise of the campsite. Somewhere there were fish in the river, and if he could catch them, then he would return the conquering hero. In the meadow, the stream split into many channels. Another stream entered the meadow. He kept moving down, looking for the right place to catch the big one.

Time seemed unimportant; there was no watch, no cell phone, nothing on the schedule. Still, after hours of fishing frustration, Jared remembered he might be missed and turned around to head back to camp. But nothing seemed familiar. He decided he needed to get back; he was not with his buddy. His scoutmaster insisted on his being with his buddy all the time. Then he worried. *I'm going to be in trouble—big trouble.*

As with many lost adolescents, Jared's primary motivation—the idea that drove his strategy—became staying out of trouble. The fear of parents, teachers, and other adults clouds immediate right action. Jared believed if he followed the river, it would take him back to the lake, but with its slow and windy pace, he could not tell for sure which way the river was flowing. He guessed wrong.

My pager went off just as we were leaving for a dinner on Friday August 12, 2011. I had awoken from a long three-hour nap after an early flight from the East Coast in the morning, so when I learned that we might be searching through the night for a missing Boy Scout, I knew I would be a little less exhausted than the others. The gear was already in the car, so I grabbed my radio, checked the GPS, and loaded Dusty in his travel crate. I headed to Evanston, Wyoming, stopping to buy extra batteries for the flashlights, and then headed toward Daggett County, Utah.

Daggett County is a small, remote county in the northeast corner of Utah. From the Wasatch Front, it is best accessed through Wyoming. About a three-hour drive from the population centers of Utah, it boasts two natural wonders that attract nature lovers, city slickers, and Boy Scouts from the Wasatch Front. The first is Flaming Gorge Reservoir, a national recreation site that forms a forty-five-mile long lake in the Green River Basin. The second is the back door to the Uintahs, a thirty- by one hundred-mile mountainous wilderness area that is the only mountain range that runs east to west in the United States.

Our instructions were to meet the sheriff and his SAR team at Spirit Lake, where these scouts had embarked on a five-mile hike to Daggett Lake. The Rocky Mountain Rescue Dog team who was coming from all points in Utah agreed to meet at the small town of McKinnon and drive the last twenty miles together. That way, we could coordinate actions and share information.

Marie was named "incident commander," a role that most of the experienced handlers had filled on various searches. Incident commanders are the contact point for the law enforcement agency that requests our services. They also formulate and execute the search strategies. Often in the hurry up of a search, there is not time to discuss the various possibilities. While incident commanders give out as much information and take input when possible, often they only have time to assign search areas and deal with essential communications.

Marie is a beautiful blonde Swedish woman who, on first glance, would not seem to be a typical search-and-rescue volunteer. While her uniform is pressed and all the badges are in perfect order, she often streaks her hair with pink or green. On a search, she is absolutely professional. For a rookie like me, it brings a sense of security to have an incident commander who is clear, direct, and helpful. Her welcoming voice is high and sometimes girlish. But Marie is a devoted mother of three teenage children. Her dog Guinness is a bloodhound-Labrador mix with exceptional tracking capabilities. She is just the right person to lead a team.

In our predeployment briefing, Marie reminded us that if we found the victim, we were to radio immediately using the bandana code. "I've found a red bandana means you have found a deceased victim," she reminded us. "I've found a yellow bandana means you have found a victim who needs medical attention. I've found a green bandana means the victim is in good condition."

She said the sheriff told us we would not search in the night but be deployed at first light in order to get ahead of the other searchers on horseback, ATV, and foot who would be descending on the area. The Daggett County Sheriff knew that if he could get our dogs in the area with relatively few other distractions, they could track the young scout.

As we drove the twenty-mile dirt road to Spirit Lake, we passed television news trucks headed down the mountain. All four Salt Lake City stations had made the missing Boy Scout their lead story on the late news. Later, this story would make regional and national news.

Lost scouts are big news in Utah. First, Boy Scouts is very popular in the family-oriented state. Most neighborhoods sponsor a troop. During the summer, the scouts pour into the mountains in search of fish, fun, and adventure. But the second reason is a community nightmare that still haunts the state. In 2006, a young scout named Garrett Bardsley was fishing with his father at Cumeranth Lake in the Uintahs. Unprepared for the cold of the morning, he told his dad that he was going back to camp to get a jacket. It was only a few hundred yards back to camp, but he was never seen again.

During a six-week period, thousands of people searched for Garrett. National news coverage and police investigations looked at all possibilities, including abduction. Searchers found hundreds of socks, shoes, fishing lines, and clothing items from other scouts, but none were connected to Garrett. Eventually, with winter coming early to the higher altitudes, the search was called off, but the incident is seared into our collective memory.

At Daggett Lake, Jared was missed almost immediately. By two o'clock in the afternoon, his scoutmaster had sent a text message to ask for help. Scouts, in groups of three, were assigned to look in obvious areas and then return and report. Adult leaders scoured the more difficult locations in a hasty search to find the missing boy. By four o'clock, sheriff's deputies had arrived in the camp, and other searchers were headed in. By six o'clock, a state helicopter with infrared capabilities was headed in. By then, Rocky Mountain Rescue Dogs, Great Basin Rescue Dogs, and other groups were on their way.

When the news of a missing scout came to Jared's hometown of Hooper, Utah, reaction was swift. The town was rooted in ranching, and many people had horses and outdoor experience to offer. The Daggett County Sherriff had already asked for a lot of assistance from groups like Rocky Mountain Rescue Dogs, but citizens of

Hooper were marshaling their own resources. Mothers of the scouts in the troop began gathering food to support the searchers. Fathers and sons, former scouts, made ready their gear. Jared's neighbors comforted the family and helped them make the three-hour drive to the search area. Optimistic, Jared's mother packed a clean set of clothes for her son to wear after he had been found.

We arrived at the field headquarters for the search about ten thirty and bedded down for the night, hoping to get a few hours of sleep before our trek into Daggett Lake. All night our sleep was interrupted by the bang and clang of horse trailers and pickup trucks coming into camp from Hooper. By dawn, more than two hundred of Jared's neighbors were in place to help find a boy who had not yet been missing for a day.

But Jared knew none of this. As the moon replaced the sun on the horizon, he wondered if he had been missed. He thought he would be in big trouble, grounded for a week, a month, or even a year! What would the scoutmaster tell his mom and dad? His emotions shifted wildly from anger to fear, faith to humility. He thought about how stupid he had been to not bring his ten essentials or stay with his buddy. He wondered if he had the right strategy going downstream until he hit a trail. He was mad at himself and sometimes mad at those who should be looking for him. *Why? Why have they not found me?* he wondered.

Then some hope—a noise, a helicopter. Jared yelled and screamed and waved. "I saw him go over me, and I stood out in the field so he could see me. I waved my arms, but he was gone somewhere else."

"Did you know why it was there?" I asked.

"Sure," he said with confidence. "I knew everyone would be looking for me. Sometimes I could hear them yelling; I just could not tell which direction the yelling was coming from." He had yelled back until he was hoarse.

For a brief time, Jared had what he called a "freak out." A toxic mix of fear, anger, and disappointment overwhelmed him. He didn't want to cry, but he couldn't help it. He thought of his mother, his father, his family, and his fellow scouts. He wondered if he would die. But most of all he worried about being in trouble. Then he came to himself and said out loud, "I can figure this out. I know what to do. Downstream, sooner or later, I'll come to a trail or road or something." But that strategy would take him farther from his scout troop and farther from where the helicopter was heading.

"Maybe I could just climb up that hill and look around. Maybe I could see the camp," he told himself. He started the climb, but he lost sight of the stream. "I didn't want to lose the only familiar landmark I had." So back down the hill he went to the familiar.

When the heat of the day had passed, the Utah Department of Transportation helicopter began making passes around Daggett Lake. Using heat-seeking technology, it could see live body mass giving off heat. Most often it identified deer and bear, moose and elk. But the helicopter computer could highlight human body shapes and alert the pilot. But the scan of Daggett Lake and surroundings yielded nothing.

By the light of the moonlit sky, Jared had continued down the drainage and was now, perhaps, four miles from camp and out of the Daggett Lake area.

After a choppy sleep, we were roused and briefed; we drove the final five miles to the trailhead. Even though it was the last week of summer, the grass was crusty with frost. I grabbed a granola bar and some water, wanting calories and hydration before what was likely to be a long search. After a careful briefing from Marie, we began our brisk hike to Daggett Lake, hoping to be able to track Jared before other scents and distractions came pouring into the area.

As we headed up the trail, some members of the team fanned out with their dogs, thinking that Jared might have been on the trail and wandered off, but the dogs did not alert and any scent, except the scent of other searchers.

A wilderness track for a good search dog is not a difficult problem, even if the trail left by the victim is eighteen hours old. When we walk, we all shed microscopic skin grafts. These are dead skin cells that our bodies replace. The skin grafts cling to bushes, trees, and grass, creating a path that leads to us. Thousands of years of evolution taught the canine family to learn to identify and follow those skin grafts. They can even tell, within a few feet, which direction offers the freshest skin rafts. For an experienced and well-trained dog like Marie's Guinness, this would be a perfect problem.

I've Found a Green Bandana

Only a mile away from our camp, along the stream, Jared was just falling asleep. After wandering well into the night, he stopped near a clump of trees, gathered some sticks, and built a shelter. The dirt was still warm from the 80-degree day, so he dug down with a stick and pulled dirt and leaves around his body. It was 34 degrees, and all he had on was his T-shirt, jeans, and tennis shoes. It had been a year since he had learned this skill in a wilderness survival merit badge class. The instructor was not sure he had paid attention. But now, in the urgency of his situation, he remembered. "The wilderness survival merit badge leader taught us last year in scout camp how to build a lean-to. Then I pulled dirt and leaves around me and tried to stay warm. Still, I was real cold."

But we were no longer in camp. After three miles of hiking, Marie asked me to hold back and wait for other team members who were arriving late. From my position on the ridge above

Daggett Lake, I could see our first team members arriving in the search area. I could hear the radio chatter asking how to best get to the scout camp and see the searchers fan out, dogs in the lead. I had stayed on the ridge to wait for two other team members, and it put me in a position to serve as a radio relay. As I waited, a team of horse riders from Hooper came up beside us. By then, ground pounders from Jared's hometown had also joined us, all ready to search the areas around the lake. The pleasant conversation and sharing of information was interrupted by a radio call from the incident command center. "We have found a green bandana."

When Jared woke up in his makeshift shelter, he was not really rested. The sun was higher in the sky, but it still felt like morning. The hunger from missing breakfast was layered on the hunger of the missing dinner. "I really wanted to get out of there," he said. He began walking again downstream. Feeling a need to cross the river, he stumbled and got a little wet.

After walking for about twenty minutes or so, he came to a dike in the stream, a man-made structure that told him he was close to civilization. There was a road, and then he heard something. "It sounded like an engine, but then it stopped. Then I heard someone yelling my name. I called back." It didn't take long for the scout and the ATV searcher to meet, and within a few minutes, Jared was in the Commend Center telling his story. A tearful reunion with his parents followed.

Will You Find Him?

When Jared went missing, he was the same age as my son John, who is also a Boy Scout. On my way out the door to search for Jared, my son John asked seriously, "Dad, are you going to find him?" John knew that many of our missions ended in finding a deceased victim. Instead of giving him the probabilities, I said with confidence, "Yes! John, we will find him." I knew that scouts learned from a young age how to deal with survival situations. I knew how much John knew about surviving in the woods. I knew that there would be hundreds of people looking in a relatively confined space.

SAR commanders face the "will you find him" question in every search. While the commander does not or cannot always share all of her information with the loved ones of the victim, there is a simple formula that's used for calculating the probability of success in a search.

Assume that a person was last seen in the middle of a square. If you cut the square into four equal search areas, then you could assume there was a 25 percent chance that the victim wandered into one of the four search areas. The commander will assign teams to cover each of the areas. Each team reports back after a day's searching and says how much of their search area they covered. If a searcher in Area 1 (25 percent of the total search area) reported 80 percent coverage, then the formula would be to multiply 80 percent by 25 percent to get a 20 percent likelihood that the victim would be found in that quadrant on that day.

Of course, there are two critical assumptions that must be true in order for this formula to work. First, the searcher needs to truly be able to say that they covered and cleared their area. The size of the area, the terrain, and the time of year can all make significant coverage difficult. Full coverage is only theoretically possible. In my searches, I have never been able to say that I was more than 70 percent sure that the victim was not in my area. Even in open desert there are mineshafts, narrow rock cracks, hidden cliffs, and other places where a person or a body can go unnoticed. Sometimes dogs are distracted or are having a bad day, like you and I might, and they miss the scent cone where the victim's scent is "visible" to their nose. It might also be winds that change direction and push the scent up instead of along the ground. Full coverage can never be claimed.

The second assumption is that the victim is in the search area. That is an assumption for the search strategist or incident commander. In a search we did for a young girl in a small Nevada town, the incident commander knew that police were conducting a criminal investigation that would more likely yield the truth than the runway-from-home scenario he was working. Sure enough, they called off the search midday and a few hours later announced the arrest of a young man who was eventually charged with murder. The young victim was not in our search area, but police did not know that for sure until they obtained a confession.

But if it is known that the victim is in the search area, if perimeters have been set up and you know that the victim is somewhere on your search map, then the first part of the above formula is based on victim behavior: where did the victim choose to go? This is unknown. The second part of the formula is based on searcher behavior: how well did you search? How difficult was the terrain? Did dogs or other tools, such as heat-seeking helicopters, help you enhance your coverage?

It is not hard to take this same formula into a broader behavioral context. In life, two major variables control whether someone is likely to be found. The first is the lost person's commitment to be found. The second is the response of the community to find the person. Recently, I watched a Japanese man's video of a tsunami. While the wave never hit the man, as it approached you could hear him say, "It is here. This is the end. It is over." It is hard to be critical of a man facing that kind of force, but his language indicates that he has a low commitment to being found, because he has already given up. I contrast this with a fourteen-year-old girl I once knew who continued to fight a losing battle with cancer. "This fight is all I have now," she told me. Many factors determine if someone will be found, but the simple answer to the question is "yes" if they have a high commitment to being found and a high-commitment community to reach out for them.

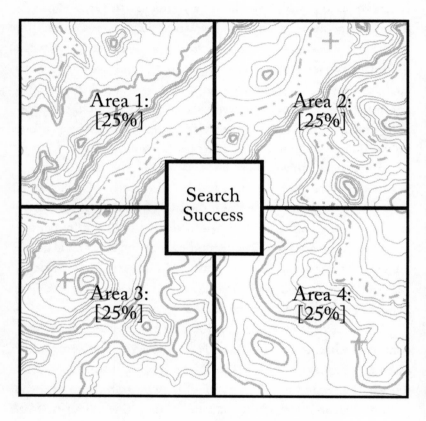

Area 1 Coverage [0–100%] x .25

Area 2 Coverage [0–100%] x .25

Area 3 Coverage [0–100%] x .25

Area 4 Coverage [0–100%] x .25

= **Probability of Find**

The High-Commitment Victim

Jared was a high-commitment victim. He made a mistake by getting lost. With that came confusion and guilt. He was flooded with self-doubt about his strategy to be found. He was full of fear. He worried that he would be in trouble, that people would be angry, and that he would not be found. But he acted as if being found was his responsibility. He pushed back the negative emotions as if to hold them for another time. He pushed back the fear and doubt. Then he identified a strategy to move downstream until he could find a trail or path. Perhaps going upstream would have been better, but he chose downstream and persisted with his plan.

Jared planned to be found within a few hours and be reunited with his troop. When that did not happen, he continued down the drainage. When he saw the moose and calf, he did not change his plan; he only waited until they passed, and then he moved on. When rescue still did not come by nightfall, he improvised a shelter and created some warmth around him. He persisted with his strategy and did not lose sight of the river. He kept moving and yelling as he could. Except for the brief "freak out," he took responsibility for his situation and tried to make it better.

When I met Jared just a few hours after being found, he was nonchalant but not cocky. "I knew I would be found," he said. "I just wanted it now."

The will to live, the ability to solve unanticipated problems, and the willingness to improvise and go around barriers increases the chance that one will be found. In 1914, Ernest Shackleton took a crew of twenty-seven men on an ill-fated expedition to become the first to cross the Antarctic. Despite the recent outbreak of World War I, the English Admiralty, headed by Sir Winston Churchill, approved the adventure.

Shackleton's men never set foot on the continent. Their ship, ironically named the Endurance, became trapped in the ice in the Weddell Sea on December 5, 1914. For the next eight months the crew survived in the trapped ship until the ice crushed the hull, leaving Shackleton and his men with three lifeboats and tons of supplies. The crew camped on the ice for several months and eventually loaded all their gear into the three lifeboats and headed through the maze of floating ice to the uninhabited Elephant Island, more than 350 miles from where the Endurance had sunk. After a five-day journey in open water, with crewmembers rowing without rest, they arrived at the island on April 6, 1916. This was the first time in 497 days that his crew had stood on solid ground. But the ground was hardly friendly. The rocky island inhabited only by seals and penguins did nothing to protect the men from the freezing winds that blew off the partially frozen sea.

Shackleton, or The Boss, as the crew called him, ordered the crew to make camp. Typical to his leadership style, he was positive, confident, and approachable. If he ever doubted the crew would be rescued, he never let on.

After settling on Elephant Island, the crew renewed their strength on a steady diet of penguin and seal. Shackleton ordered the ship's Captain Frank Worsley and a carpenter named NcNeish to modify the strongest of the lifeboats to be readied for an open sea journey. The plan was to sail eight hundred miles northeast to the South Georgia Island whaling station where he would secure a rescue ship for his men.

On April 24, 1916, Shackleton set out on one of the most precarious sea journeys ever recorded. With Frank Worsley navigating and just four weeks' worth of supplies onboard, he and five others took to the sea. For fifteen days, the roughest ocean in the world tossed about the boat. Shackleton writes: "The eighth, ninth, and tenth days of the voyage had few features worthy of special note. The wind blew hard during those days, and the strain of navigating the boat was unceasing; but always we made some advance toward our goal. No bergs showed on our horizon, and we knew that we were clear of the ice fields. Each day brought its little round of troubles, but also compensation in the form of food and growing hope. We felt that we were going to succeed. The odds against us had been great, but we were winning through. We still suffered severely from the cold, for, though the temperature was rising, our vitality was declining owing to shortage of food, exposure, and the necessity of maintaining our cramped positions day and night. I found that it was now absolutely necessary to prepare hot milk for all hands during the night in order to sustain life till dawn."

By miracle, luck, and navigational genius they arrived at South Georgia Island in the middle of a hurricane-like storm. They were within reach of land but had to stay away from the coast the night of the hurricane because they could not see a safe place to go ashore. During a short break in the weather, they made it safely ashore and then realized that the whaling station on was on the other side of the island and between them stood a range of glacier-capped mountains.

Beset by a tsunami-sized wave, extreme thirst, and sea-soaked food, Shackleton took stock. "The bright moments were those when we each received our one mug of hot milk during the long, bitter watches of the night. Things were bad for us in those days, but the end was coming. The morning of May 8 broke thick and stormy, with squalls from the north-west."

On the wrong side of South Georgia Island, they sheltered beneath the boat while they recovered their strength for the overland trek. "We would take three days' provisions for each man in the form of sledging ration and biscuit. The food was to be packed in three socks, so that each member of the party could carry his own supply. Then we were to take the Primus lamp filled with oil, the small cooker, the carpenter's adze (for use as an ice-axe), and the alpine rope, which made a total length of fifty feet when knotted."

With a fifty-foot length of rope and nails the carpenter affixed to their boots for hiking on the ice, Shackleton and two others scaled the peaks and found the whaling station. It would be another forty years before anyone else would record a crossing on that hostile geography. Stumbling into the whaling station after thirty-six hours of hiking, Shackleton went right to the headquarters. Unrecognizable from more than two years of exposure, hunger, fatigue, and hardship, he had to convince the Norwegian whalers that he was, in fact, the same Ernest Shackleton who had visited the faraway community almost two years earlier.

Quickly, a boat was dispatched to pick up the three others on the far side of the island. It would be another three months and three attempts before Shackleton would rescue his remaining crew on Elephant Island. But all twenty-eight of them survived to return to a hero's welcome in England.

You can debate whether Shackleton erred in planning his ill-fated expedition. You can argue that his ego blurred his vision and contributed to putting his men in harm's way. He died several years later at the same whaling station on South Georgia Island on his way to yet another Antarctic expedition. But you cannot argue that his contagious will to live was heroic. Without his encouragement, insight, experience, and plan, all would have perished. He sponsored talent shows while his crew sat trapped in the ice, requiring all members to participate. He gave his only mittens to Captain Frank Worsley, who had lost his while traveling to Elephant Island. He kept a clear head and positive outlook at all times, according to his companions, even when a mountain range stood between him and the hope of rescue.

The Temperament and Character Inventory used by trait theory psychologists did not exist at the time of Shackleton, but surely he would have scored exceptionally high on the persistence scale. He had an eagerness that pushed his effort to the extreme, beyond what anyone had ever endured on an Antarctic expedition. He was work hardened, and he asked others with particular skills to join him. But he also put himself at risk before he asked others. It was Shackleton who took the precarious over-ocean voyage. It was Shackleton who led out over the mountains. He was also a perfectionist. He settled for nothing but the best. He wanted every man to return home.

Not everyone has Shackleton's persistence, but Jared did. Sue and Ray Baird did. But some, unfortunately, would score in negative numbers.

In the spring we were called to do a search of a large island in the middle of the Great Salt Lake. The terrain was rough, rocky, and open. We searched beaches and coves, cliffs and trails. The victim had been missing for three days. He was despondent, but we were told he was unarmed. Because we are a volunteer organization, Rocky Mountain Rescue Dogs will not deploy when the victim might be armed. None of us have the training or experience to deal with situations where guns are involved. This young man, we were told, did not want to be found. A few days after our search ended, his body washed ashore, the victim of a self-inflicted gunshot. After his body was recovered, we learned that he had been the subject of a search just three weeks earlier in another county. Six months prior to that, he had triggered yet another search. In both the previous searches, he had wandered into difficult terrain, hoping to separate permanently from his community. He wanted to not be found. This tragic young man without commitment to be found also came from a community that did not care.

The High-Commitment Community

High-commitment victims like Jared are most likely to be found when they come from a high-commitment community. Once an isolated small town, Hooper is now surrounded by urban encroachment, but it has not lost its small town values. Not everyone is part of the dominant political party. Not everyone goes to the same church. But everyone is part of the community.

In a community like Hooper, helping the helpless is a knee-jerk reaction. There is no hesitancy. It comes from generations of hard times in the depression, a recession, or when pioneers were first farming the land. The generations speak out and speak into hearts and remind us all that we have been in need. In such a community, the official response is never enough. It is never just the sheriff's problem or that of the search-and-rescue team. It is never a problem for strangers and volunteers. Everyone is a volunteer. Everyone works together. People who grew up in such a community know no other way. Those who did not are suspicious of the instant kindness and dubious of the motives.

For Jared, the will to live might have been enough to save him. Eventually, he would have reached the road and flagged down a car. But in the best cases, the lost person and the community reach together—one admitting that they have deviated and separated, another saying with open arms, "Come home. All is forgiven." Every community is something less when someone is lost. Every community invests so much in a child or an adult, in his education, career, value, and humanity. People in places that do not seek their lost members are no longer communities. They are suburbs, developments, and complexes. They are places to live—but they are not communities.

How can you tell if you are part of a community? A community helps when someone says, "I have found a yellow bandana." A community mourns when someone says, "I found a red bandana." And a community rejoices when someone says, "I found a green bandana."

As we arrived at the trailhead after our search for Jared, even though our efforts did not lead to his rescue, his family, his friends, his fellow scouts, and his community welcomed us and cheered. They gave us water, petted our dogs, and offered food and deep gratitude.

If you are lost in the woods overnight or lost in the morass of drug or alcohol abuse, it is hard to feel like you are not alone. In the dark of a moonlit forest, all remembrance of others is dulled, and the immediacy of your aloneness dominates. If you want to be found, do what Jared and others who make it out do: visualize the love of others. You are never lost alone. Somewhere, someone is looking. Some are your loved ones; some are strangers who have been lost themselves. All want to bring you home.

An early morning page woke me up on a Saturday morning in late June 2013. Our K-9 search team was being called to the Monte Cristo area of Northern Utah to search for an 8 year-old boy who had been missing overnight. The young boy had gone camping with a church group. While the adults built a campfire, the young boys walked 200 yards to a ridge and collected snow from a drift to make snowballs, hoping to ambush the adults. Since this young boy's father was not available, his neighbor brought him along with his sons for what was loosely called a "father and sons activity." The subject of the search made it to the snowdrift, but on the way home, he got turned around and headed unnoticed in the wrong direction.

I had the longest drive of any of the team members, and got caught behind construction zones several times. When I arrived at the high altitude Command Center my team had already deployed, and when the young boy was found an hour later, I was in a far part of the search area. I was the last searcher out and the last one in.

Dirty and sweaty when I walked into camp, most of the team had left. The Rich County Search and Rescue Team was dismantling the Command Center, and a young woman who I had never seen was standing on the side of the road waiting for me. She was the mother of the boy. "She approached and without hesitation embraced me. "Thank-you! Thank-you," she said. "I really didn't do anything," I said, but she would not let her appreciation go unheard.

I asked her how her son was found. "When it got dark, he got really scared. He prayed, but he was still scared, so he prayed again and again. After five times, he decided to go out in the middle of a nearby field where he might be seen. He said there was a big pile of grass in the field, so he climbed in and fell asleep."

In the morning, several horseback riders came through the area and saw the boy asleep in the hay and brought him home. "He's no different than if he slept in his bed at home," his mother said.

Years later, when he told about the final push three exhausted men made over the unmapped mountains of South Georgia Island, Ernest Shackleton wrote, "I know that during the long and racking march of thirty-six hours over the unnamed mountains and glaciers of South Georgia it seemed to me often that we were four, not three. I said nothing to my companions on the point, but afterward Worsley said to me, 'Boss, I had a curious feeling on the march that there was another person with us.' Crean confessed to the same idea. One feels 'the dearth of human words, the roughness of mortal speech' in trying to describe things intangible, but a record of our journeys would be incomplete without a reference to a subject very near to our hearts."

Use the CR code scanner on your smart phone to watch
"Winter Camp Training," a three-minute video by the author.
(Also available at LessonsoftheLost.com)

Chapter 9:

Some Small Things Matter, and Some Big Things Don't

On June 20th, 2013, 61-year old James Randy Udall went for a weeklong solo-backpacking trip in Wyoming's Wind River Range. He had hiked in this most pristine mountain range in the continental United States on many occasions, often going off trail to find new roots and encounter the raw wilderness.

Randy Udall was an environmentalist. He helped establish the Community Office for Resource Energy Efficiency, which promotes the use of renewable energy. His family has a long history in western politics. Cousin Tom Udall is a U.S. Senator from Arizona. His uncle, Stewart Udall, was Secretary of the Interior in the 1960's. He did not just love the wilderness in the west, he lived it.

So when he did not return at the appointed time and place, a massive search was launched. Hundreds of people came from all over the west. Members of our Rocky Mountain Rescue team were inserted on the peaks and high points by helicopter, each one taking a drainage and covering carefully as their dogs checked everything human in the giant patch of primitive green.

It was just a small thing that resolved the search, just a little detail that seemed unimportant when surrounded by the hundreds or thousands of details that flood into any search. A ground searcher found a footprint by a stream in one of the search areas. He did not recognize it. It looked to be a week or so old. That night he reported his clue to the Incident Commander.

In a search this large, the Incident Commander takes in hundreds of clues each day. They process them by priority, sorting them by significance, and hope a pattern will emerge. It is tedious work that takes most of the night, but from it emerges an informed search strategy for the next day.

The next morning, my Rocky Mountain Rescue Dog colleague, Dee Dilman, boarded a helicopter to be ferried into a search area. The previous day he had spent 14 hours clearing high mountain meadows, and he was tired. But the search was still new enough that there was some hope for a good resolution, so searchers were pushing themselves and their dogs. As Dee boarded the craft, the pilot asked him to "keep his eyes out on the way up." They planned to fly over the area where an unidentified footprint had been found the previous day. Just a small clue that they could check out and check off the list.

As they flew up and over the trees nearing the top of the drainage, Dee saw the flash of a bright red nylon coat in an open space below him. He cranked his neck, and as he did, his dog Pastis alerted. It just takes a small thing, something so small that humans can't see it or smell it. A skin cell or gases that come from human decomposition blowing in the wind, and the dog instinctively barks. In a helicopter, flying above a body, Pastis told him that there were human remains below him. "It stands to reason," Dee later said, "That the helicopter passing over would kick up the scent and my dog would get a nose full."

Struggling to find the microphone, Dee alerted the pilot, who landed as close as they could to the body. Just a "small thing," and then another small thing, that lead to a big thing.

According to the National Association for Search and Rescue (NASAR), a lost person is "a known individual in an unknown location whose safety may be threatened by conditions related to environment, the weather, or to the age or health factors of concern to family or caregivers." (NASAR, 2004) This wilderness searcher definition works well for those lost in work or life, because it underscores the change in the environment, the threat of danger, and the relationship to loved ones. From the perspective of the lost person, the things that threaten us first appear as insignificant. They are small factors that are easily dismissed.

This definition also does not describe the problem in the mind and the heart of the lost person, where your inner compass is spinning and your mental maps are failing. Being lost is an internal problem first. Often it takes a blinding snowstorm, a layoff, a divorce, an illness, or a death to help us see that our inner compass and mental maps are insufficiently guiding us through our changing environments. Often, suddenly we become aware that the world around us floods our senses with data but no apparent meaning, with physical and emotional needs but no comfort, with ideas but no clear actions. In other words, being lost is more than being in the wrong place; it is being in the wrong state of mind.

When mental maps become mental traps, orienting with just the external compass may make things better, but it does not solve the problem. Sometimes environmental conditions change quickly, and our grip on what worked in the past remains fast. In those cases, a wrong action or no action can begin a chain of events that could be fatal. Rarely is the first mistake fatal. The first mistake is "small." But the second or the third mistake can end a career, ruin a relationship, fracture a family, or lead searchers to a recovery and not a rescue.

Survivors first identify where they went wrong. They don't obsess on it, and they don't punish themselves for making a mistake or having an accident. They simply take steps to turn that chain of events around so that it does not become fatal. It takes deep introspection, but most can identify a seemingly insignificant event—an error of the external compass—that led to the breakdown of the inner compass and an almost fatal event.

Victoria Grover identified that point in her conversation with the hotel clerk. "I assumed he was taking me seriously," she said. Rita Chretien identified that point when she fell asleep in after getting gas in Boise. She believed if she had helped with navigation that perhaps Al would not have driven into the remote areas of Nevada. Sue Baird identified that point when she realized that the assumption that the online mapping service she used was correct. Once she let go of that assumption, she came face-to-face with her lostness, and that was the first step toward being found. But such realizations do not always come on time.

The Mother and Daughter Reunion

The Deseret News, a Salt Lake City newspaper, ran the following story on October 15, 2007:

> Search and rescue crews were expected to return Monday morning to the High Uintahs in search of two out-of-state women who did not return home from a Utah vacation. Carole Wetherton, 58, of Panacea, Fla., and her daughter, Kim Beverly, 40, of Tucker, Ga., were supposed to board

a Saturday night flight to return home. But neither of them made the plane and family members called Utah authorities, the Summit County Sheriff's Office told KSL-TV. The women's rented sport-utility vehicle was found near the Crystal Lake trailhead Sunday afternoon. Inside the vehicle were maps and notes believed to have been day hike plans, according to the sheriff's office.

The mother and daughter had set off from the trailhead for a three-mile hike. After being cautioned by a ranger about an impending storm, they bought light windbreakers and a few supplies before driving to Washington Lake in the Uinta Mountains of Utah. The easy access from the car may have misled them into thinking that this hike, starting at ten thousand feet, was going to be easy.

Based on the notes left in the car, the two women knew that a winter storm would hit a few hours after their planned return time. They were in the "warm before the storm," which caused them to leave some clothing in the car. This was their first mistake, but the trail was a simple, direct shot to the lake up over a three hundred-foot rise.

I assume that the first part of their hike was lovely. It is a trail I have hiked many times, beginning in a thick wood that crosses streams and meadows. In the fall the browns in the grassy meadows would have complemented the yellows and oranges in the aspen trees. As you climb the few switchbacks over the hill, you rise above the timberline, and you can see a panoramic view of the Uintahs. Trial Lake and Washington Lake are visible to the east, and once over the hill, you can see Lightning Lake and the Provo River drainage.

But then the terrain changes. The country opens up, with few trees and large boulders. The trail is harder to distinguish, because in places the hard rocks form a smooth surface, almost like crossing a series of large, paved tennis courts. Rock piles mark the trail in places, but between those piles you are left to guess if you are headed in the right direction. It is easy to not notice on the way down the split in the trail that leads north. Most hikers are on their way to the lake just a mile away and clearly visible in this open country.

We know that Kim Beverly and Carole Wetherton made it to the lake, where they ate and drank. Photos showed that they took pictures posing on high boulders and smiling for the camera. Haunting reality was there for anyone to see. With each photo, the sky became darker, the clouds closer, and the environment more threatening. Still their smiles persisted in each shot. They could not see the small thing that was becoming large and coming toward them.

At some time, the searchers assume that the pair was alerted to the changes in the environment so evident in the photos and headed for the car. It was only three miles away, just over an hour on foot. They knew the route. They were in good shape—no worries.

What happened next is speculation. They probably became lost on their way back up the trail in the open country where there aren't trees to guide you to stay on the right trail and where rock piles mark the open sections. We assume that a quick snow squall might have hidden the trail. We can also assume that by the time their outer compass had failed, their inner compasses had failed too. When the women did not return to their car, the U.S. Forest Service and Summit County Search and Rescue responded. Since the notes on the car pointed to Lightning Lake, the searchers concentrated on the area for three weeks until the snow was too deep. They brought in a helicopter with infrared signature capability to look for body heat in the snow. They spent hundreds, maybe thousands, of hours in difficult conditions searching the base of rocks and trees at the headwaters of the Provo River. Frustrated by the lack of success, and pushed out of the Uinta Mountains by the winter conditions, the search was finally abandoned.

In the spring, the Summit County Search and Rescue team developed a new theory. In their original search strategy, they had assumed that the pair had encountered snow on their return trip and left the trail. The radical change in the environment would have limited their visibility. The new theory suggested that the pair had indeed stayed on the trail but had made a wrong turn. When they approached the split in the trail, they either didn't see it or didn't know which way to go. The theory presupposed they took the wrong way but continued because they were on a trail. So just a mile from the car in the winter's first storm, they diverted to the north fork trail and headed deeper into the woods and away from their original destination. Unable to see their context and blinded by the snow, they kept their faces down and stayed on the wrong trail for four miles. The small things, the weather, the clothes in the car, the wrong turn—all of which would be inconveniences in normal circumstances—combined to become fatal. Multiple small things can be more consequential than a single big thing.

It is impossible to know how they felt as they pushed down the trail. Perhaps for a while they were sure that the car was just a few feet away. We cannot know if they were ashamed for leaving their coats and maps in the car, but I believe that they thought about that and a thousand other things as they struggled to understand the meaning of their rapidly changing environment. We do know that they went off the trail a few hundred yards where they could not be seen by rescuers. They built a makeshift shelter, and they died.

The following spring, a group of searchers, including Rocky Mountain Rescue Dogs, tried to bring closure to this tragedy. Searcher Cindy Kinsman of Rocky Mountain Rescue Dogs found shreds of an emergency blanket that led her to the remains. The investigation concluded that the pair had died of exposure within twenty-four hours of leaving the car. Surely, they died wondering where they were, why they could not find the car, and what would be the best next step. The mostly downhill hike to the car, the familiarity of the terrain, and the warm before the storm had all collapsed when winter white radically changed their environment.

The Internal and External Compass

William Syrotuck, who has researched lost person behavior over forty years, helps us understand how people behave when they are lost in the wilderness. His research has strong implications for all kinds of lost. Syrotuck observed that, "People are social animals surrounded by a complex artificial environment. In the technology of today, few people are self-sufficient."

Syrotuck's research concludes that most of us are not very good at being found. We overlook big things and obsess on the small thing or fail to see the significance in something minute yet very important. We might wander for miles and never really go anywhere, burning up valuable energy in search of a direction. We might stay put and wait to be found when no one is looking for us. We might go right when left is the better course. Most importantly, Syrotuck describes how people who are lost have a variety of reactions, but all suffer some kind of shock. He says even healthy and secure people who are found within a reasonable time experience psychological trauma. I know this because even when we were lost for just thirty minutes in a whiteout on a mountain, my inner compass was spinning, my mental maps had failed, and I felt the deep shame of a newly discovered imposter.

A former student, who now has my deepest admiration, got lost in the city with his family while at work. (I share this story with his permission.) At age twenty-six, he had everything going in the right direction in his life. He had a good job, a very supportive wife, and two wonderful kids. In 2007, he started my class in the fall on his way to an April graduation. Then he dropped out, and I did not see him for two years. Where did he go? Why? What had happened? My phone calls were not returned.

After two years, he returned to my class. In an essay, he shared this story. Mark (pseudonym) had dropped out because of a small thing. A friend took him to a party. He took a drink for the first time in his life, and he could not stop. Within a year, he had moved through the hierarchy of substances to heroin. Still, he was mostly successful in hiding the addiction. As with many addicts, the internal and external compasses were malfunctioning in sync.

The day I lost my job, my wife called me up and asked me to come home for a family meeting. It seemed strange, but I got home, and I walked into the living room. My wife and children and her parents were there. For the next two hours, they described how my addiction was hurting them and destroying the family. I fought every word. It was my life. I could do what I wanted. Then they said if I continued on this track I would have no family.

They gave me two paths. The first was no job, no family, and no future. The second included rehab, counseling, and support. I took the second, but it meant radical change. I had to learn to be honest with myself and admit that I was a junkie. I had to be honest and admit that I was hurt. I had to be honest and admit that I could not do this on my own.

I was lost. I didn't know what it meant at the time, but I was lost.

Understanding that he was lost was the first step toward being found. As with most, Mark took courageous steps forward only to fall on his face. In his case, he got up and is still getting up every day to face the hole in his soul that he thought only drugs could fill.

Mark, and many others like myself, learned valuable lessons while lost. In the reorienting of the internal and external compass, we find life's most important truths. These truths are often simple, profound, and essential if we want to survive and eventually thrive in the wilderness, work, or life.

I wish I could say that all was well with Mark. He has, for the most part, stayed clean and sober. He has completed a prestigious graduate program. He is with his family and working at a good job. But several times during his recovery he took steps back that could have killed him. He fell off the wagon and then turned around, ran, and got back on it again.

"Every one of the friends I made in rehab," he told me, "are dead. They tried, but the pressure was too much. After being clean for a few months, they lost their tolerance for the drug but did not lose their appetite. The next dose killed them."

In previous chapters, I have written about the tipping point of the survival zone. In that survival state, we are so close to the edge, so close to the uncontrolled fall, so close to death, that one small thing that is insignificant in other environments can push us over the edge.

Chapter 10:

Fear Can Kill You

When we write the scripts that carry the future of our lives, we almost never put in the part about being lost. Life insurance sales people have the same problem. No one plans to die—or at least we don't talk or think about it much. No one plans to get lost either. The script of your life written in your mind does not read, "College, good career, married, children, lose job, lose wife, lose family, have fun in later years." It is more likely to have an optimistic picture. The script of my life did not include "watch brother-in-law self destruct, help him without result, be surprised when he goes missing, help organize search, search for five weeks, tell wife brother-in-law is dead, attend funeral." But that is what happened. I never imagined that the first real search with my dog would be for a member of my own family.

Searching for Hope

David always wanted to be famous, but not like this. He wanted to make a movie, write a best-selling novel, produce a top-ten song, or publish poetry. He wanted to build museums and theme parks. He wanted his children to go to the best schools and be great athletes. Unfortunately, as for many, his appetite for fame and recognition did not match his talent and opportunities. He did help build two museums, and he wrote unpublished novels, poems, and songs. But none brought him the fame and fortune he craved.

I did not know David as a child; when I married his older sister, David was already happily married with two children. He had a solid job and a stable family. Later they added two more children. His family was the center of his universe. David went to all the ball games and the children's activities. He was a good father and a good citizen.

David's career was also enviable. He was a fund-raiser for a large university, and he met regularly with the academic elite and the rich and famous. This whetted his appetite for his own success.

In the early years of our marriage, my wife and I associated with her brother's family regularly. After the birth of our first child, we asked David and his wife to be responsible for our daughter's care should anything ever happen to us.

A few years later, to our surprise, David went through the legal process of changing his last name to that of a different relative. Because he no longer shared the same name, he was separated from his brothers and sisters. Then it began to become clear that he was struggling at work. Promotions and coveted assignments did not come. We could see that he was becoming more isolated. On the rare occasions that we saw him, he complained bitterly about his job. He often described how this person or that person had personally challenged and attacked him, depriving him of deserved recognition. Eventually, he separated from his career and began a series of unfulfilling jobs that each ended after a few months. In our rare conversations, he would tell me that he wanted to be a songwriter, a Hollywood scriptwriter, or a producer. But that is hard enough to do in Hollywood, let alone in Utah. We began to see David deviate from his career and family and want to "go it alone."

During this time, David pulled me into a consulting project, overpromising money and success. After a few meetings with a client, it was clear to me that neither of us had the experience to provide what the client really needed, so I referred the client to a friend with the appropriate expertise. David was livid. He felt betrayed even though we had nothing to offer. "I need the money," he told me. "Right now I'm worth more dead than alive."

Further separation occurred as our children grew. David seemed to have a competitive drive to have "the best kids." Children from both families had special and different talents, but David wanted to engage in talk that seemed to channel his own ambitions through his children. On occasion, we began to see a deep fear in David as he spoke of his anger about getting low-level jobs and then losing them. There were conspiracies followed by further drives to competitiveness.

When David was in his forties, we saw very little of him. He had "started his own business" and was "developing projects." His elderly parents, who were under our care at the time, would tell us about David's important meetings with Hollywood producers. They described how he was about to make it big. They would also talk about how his wife was holding him back, insisting that he take an ordinary job to support the family. They also gave him money.

The illusion of importance further separated David from his family. After his father's death, we learned that his supportive father had given much of his small estate to David for his projects. We also learned that David was divorcing and would likely be moving to Hollywood. We knew that on occasion he flew to Los

Angeles, but we passed off the stories of dating superstars and working with Steven Spielberg as just harmless lies. Looking back now, I realize that he was intentionally or unintentionally trying to further separate from his family and community and deviate from their values.

As we continued to associate with his children and his former wife, David became angry. At one point when David, my wife, and their siblings met at a restaurant to discuss their mother's deteriorating health, David yelled at the group, climbed out of the booth, crawled over the table, and stormed out of the restaurant. It was a public scene that left a scar on everyone.

It was clear that David, now middle-aged, was living in a pool of anger, denial, and self-pity. He was manufacturing artificial hope with fantasy and claims of self-importance. We began to wonder how he was supporting himself until we found that he had spent his retirement and his half of the assets received in the divorce and was now borrowing money from relatives. The borrowing speech often came with an outlandish tale about a large sum of money held in a London bank that would be available to fund his projects if he could just get five or ten thousand dollars to an attorney.

After a few years, David was completely out of money. When his mother died, the wheels, already loose, came off. David was the youngest child; she had a special relationship with and very high expectations for her son. Her death signaled the final point of separation from his family, though he continued to see his children, who patiently maintained a relationship.

David told us that he was living with friends, but we later learned that he was living in his car. He began selling off family heirlooms, including paintings and jewelry inherited from his family's early life in Alaska.

In the summer of 2009, we had helped him secure a small apartment. By this time, we had realized that David was seriously ill. His two sisters and one of his brothers, along with his former wife, now five years divorced, continued to encourage him to get help, get medication, and get a basic job. His children circled him like angels. While David occasionally worked jobs in retail and telephone sales, he did not work regularly and routinely went without basic food and shelter. Most offers for help were met with anger and refusal. His anger would spill over to his ex-wife, and other times he would beg us to help him reconcile—to "fix" his life.

It did not surprise us that our invitations to Thanksgiving dinner in the fall of 2009 went unanswered. We learned that David's ex-wife had invited David to join her and their children for Thanksgiving dinner. We later learned that he did not show up. Within a few days, police checked his apartment and found it clean with a copy of the rental agreement and a set of keys on the table. His car was gone.

Later we learned that just before he left, David had his car repaired and inspected. He bought new tires and mailed checks to all his creditors. We surmised that David believed he was about to get a large sum of money and that his checks would clear. No money was transferred into his account.

Between Thanksgiving and Christmas, David was reported missing, but it was clearly an intentional departure, and police could do little. We were encouraged in January that David's car had been sighted, but it was not until late June when the high mountain snows melted that we learned that his car had been sighted on a high mountain pass on a dirt road above ten thousand feet.

In May, Sheriff's deputies and U.S. Forest Service rangers completed a hasty search using a grid pattern. They found two blankets known to be David's 150 feet from the car. All of David's belongings except his wallet and his cell phone were in the car.

Everything he owned was in an old Jeep Wagoner with new tires. In a searcher's logic, investigators and family developed three scenarios. First, he could have been despondent over another failed business deal or another failed relationship and deliberately drove to a high point to commit suicide. Cleaning up the apartment and going to a high point are both common behaviors in the profiles of suicide victims. But David had never been violent, never owned a gun, and did not, as far as we knew, have medications. Because of that, we assumed that suicide was unlikely.

The second scenario had David despondent and careless but not suicidal. He was driving over the pass and got stuck in the seven to ten inches of snow that capped Duchesne Ridge just before Thanksgiving. When the car got stuck, David grabbed his two blankets for warmth and tried to walk out. This scenario could not explain why one of David's blankets was folded neatly at the foot of one of the hills.

The third scenario was that David abandoned his car to make it look as if he were lost, and then, with an associate, started a new life with a new name somewhere else. While it seemed deceptive, it was also a hopeful scenario for the family. A similar and more likely version combined the second and third scenarios and had David walking out and being picked up along one of the roads or highways. With the opportunity before him, he then decided to start a new life.

His family and the police thought that the first or second scenario was by far the most likely and that his remains were somewhere on or near Duchesne Ridge.

As David's family and friends saw him as he began to separate, the deviation before Thanksgiving was not surprising, so few were surprised when his car was found. The most common concern from friends, family, and children was about the point of realization. When did David know he was lost?

Realization too Late

Of course, our point of realization came much earlier. We were all willing to point our fingers at David and say, "You are lost." We were all willing to reach out but to a point—we wanted David to take over a realistic navigation of his own life. We loved David, but we loved him imperfectly, and so we shared some of his fate.

In the earlier chapters, I mentioned how the point of realization is often crippling because it can amplify the already unmanageable fear, but the point of depravation is often fatal. Unless there is outside intervention, it is unlikely that someone will be saved.

I have argued throughout this book that being lost is about losing meaning to the point where there is no hope. This is where David was. With literally hundreds of hands reaching out to help, he chose to walk into the woods and end his life in suicide by radical neglect.

After the car was located, the skilled SAR team from Wasatch County advised that we wait a few weeks and let snow fully melt before a search. With family not willing to wait, many of my dear friends from within the search community organized to help. With expert tracking, area-scent dogs, and experienced searchers, we went over the high-probability areas several times. We followed the roads out, searching within several hundred yards. We searched all the key drainages. It was a vast territory.

After ten days of searching over five weeks, the Wasatch Country SAR team joined us with a team of cadaver dogs from Carbon County. Again, the high-probability areas were searched, as were lower-probability areas. Hundreds of clues were explored, such as an abandoned tent, a knife, snowmobile parts, and animal bones.

Finally, in the late afternoon on the day of our final push, the cadaver dog team asked the SAR commander and me for advice.

I suggested that the team enter the high-probability search area at a different angle, hoping that something different would be seen. The team went down the hill and up onto a ridge. Others had been on the ridge with dogs, but this time the wind was blowing in a different direction.

The dog team descended from the ridge, veering east. As they came up over a second ridge, the first dog alerted, then the second, then all five. Their noses went up. They started driving into the wind, down the ridge, and into a streambed, following the scent. About a mile and a half from where he left the car, they found his remains, some clothing, and a note. It began with, "My name is David …"

The find triggered a crime scene investigation and police activities where I could not help. So I packed up my gear and drove northeast, along highway and dirt road, all the time trying to compose the words I would use to tell my wife that we found her brother, face down in a stream, having committed suicide by neglect. In his last moments, he was alone, cold, despondent, and crushed.

Often the survivors turn on searchers. My friend Reverend Dean Jackson, who served as a police chaplain, told me how in some of the death notifications he had delivered he was often seen as the cause of the tragedy. "Sometimes they need someone to blame, and they blame you because you are the stranger who brought them this terrible news."

I was not a stranger, but one of the hardest things I have ever done is tell my wife how we found her brother. It was expected but still very hard. But she made it easy, thanking me and thanking me again for my small role in the search. In those moments and days after the find, we prepared a funeral involving family members and friends. On the surface, everyone was somber, kind, and appropriate. But underneath, I could see that this kind of death brings anger and fear. There was anger toward David for putting his family through so much, anger toward those who helped find him and those who delivered the bad news, and anger toward the sheriff and others for not finding him soon enough.

Fear also brought a toxic bitterness. How much are we like David? Could this happen again? Could it happen to one of our children? To this day, some branches of the family tree still shake when they think of David.

A Wilderness of His Own Making

When I first started doing search work, I naively thought every lost person wanted to be found. I pictured in my mind the survivors on a desert island spelling out "SOS" on the sand, or people lost in the woods building a smoky fire to signal a plane. I pictured a crying child wanting to be reunited with her mother. I carry a whistle on the zipper of every backpack so I can always get to it. It travels farther than a human voice and does not get hoarse from yelling for help. It is the best low-tech tool for being found. Three blasts, and rescuers know where you are. I also now carry a Spot GPS locator, GPS, compass, map, and survival gear. If I am lost, I want to be found.

But most people don't cry for help. They don't. Some don't even bother to tell anyone they are going to go missing. They just walk. That's what David did. With his remains, was a note, but there was no indication why he did what he did. I personally believe that he committed suicide. Not active, decisive suicide with death by gunshot, overdose, or some other morbid yet effective way, but suicide by neglect, by pushing others away and away until isolation and deprivation was fatal. He walked away from life, loved ones, and reality. He walked into the woods. When he stopped walking, he was already dead. His self-made wilderness was too profound, too deep, and too dark; the actual winter wilderness at high altitude seemed like a better place to be.

Many lost people do not even know they are lost. They deny their state and manage to continue to do enough to survive but not thrive. For a long time David was in this state. He was right, and the world was wrong. He wondered why when he deviated and separated that his family and work colleagues did not follow. This leads to deep isolation and a dense weight of fear that drags, divides, and immobilizes.

Fear is a toxic brick that poisons and blinds. It is heavy, weighing down every step and blurring every decision. For the lost, fear can be fatal. There are many kinds of fear. I see the fear of incompetence paralyze innovation in business and higher education. When professors who have spent their lives mastering the theoretical aspects of a subject are then asked to engage their classes in a community project where success is measured by different standards, they fear being seen by their students as being incompetent. Sometimes doctors fear that referring a patient to another doctor will make them look like someone less.

Fear of intimacy often plagues youth, though it can hit anyone from any generation. Not the hormone-driven, physical intimacy but the intimacy that comes when relationships become deep, trust is profound, and words can be anticipated. It is the kind of intimacy generated only by personal, deep, long, and honest dialogue. It rarely, if ever, comes though the cluttered communications mediated by Internet, cell phone, or text message.

Fear of irrelevance is a toxic pit for older adults, particularly men, who want to leave their marks in this world. But fear of scarcity is the most toxic of fears. When you don't have enough love, enough food, enough clean water, enough information, enough air, you will do things and become things that you never would suspect. The fear of scarcity drives wars and personal conflicts. It drives greed. It pushes children out of the home and couples into divorce. It is the cause of most work conflicts.

The Searcher's Dilemma

So if a person does not want to be found or does not know he is lost, then how will he behave differently when searchers come to find him? Many experienced search-and-rescue workers have stories of finding a victim after a long three- or four-day search, and the victim denies being lost. In his heart the person knows he is lost, but the denial is a tactic to avoid criticism or preserve dignity. He might reluctantly accept a helicopter ride or an escort to safety but never really admits in public that he is lost. It is unlikely that he will express appreciation, and it is more likely that he will criticize the searchers in an effort to deflect the attention away from his own incompetence.

Most searchers I know are ready for this. While appreciation is reciprocal, in most cases we just search and go home with hardly a thanks or even a word from the people we helped. But if you are a parent, a boss, a spouse, or a friend trying to help someone who does not think that she is lost, then you have a different problem. You are trying to move this person into the want-to-be-rescued category so that there is an acknowledgement of the situation and a willingness to accept help. Do you wait until there is acknowledgement? Do you let things get so bad that there is a felt need for change? Do you help and hope that the help brings about a realization and triggers self-help and personal responsibility?

We have a moral responsibility as searchers to look for people and help them be rescued even if they do not acknowledge the need or want the help. Our efforts are likely to be imperfect. We might also be limited in the success we can achieve. But we must reach out. There are too many people who test the caring capacity of their social networks by moving toward the I-don't-want-to-be-found box. If we don't reach out and pull them back, even when they deny the need or don't fully accept the help, then their situations may deteriorate to the point where they might fall into that fatal category of not wanting to be found.

As a parent, I am glad that I continued to reach for my daughter, though my efforts were far from perfect. When Becky was in her early teens, we began to see the mood swings experienced by most teenagers. As she was our first child, we did not realize at first that Becky seemed to visit sadness more often and stay longer than others. We knew she was brilliant, but we also knew that she had difficulty finishing assignments, turning work in, and fitting in in highly structured environments.

Becky was a devoted reader who had always excelled in English and writing. She had already read most of the classics before entering high school. Yet teachers told us that she was often inattentive in class and sometimes disruptive. Often she turned assignments in late. Sometimes she did not turn them in at all.

On one occasion during her sophomore year, an English teacher called our home to complain about an incident that we found quite amusing. The teacher reported that she had turned the class over to a young student teacher who was teaching a modal on Shakespeare's *Romeo and Juliet*. The young teacher, who was likely trying to impress her mentor more than she was trying to teach the students, saw that Becky was talking to her friend in the back of the class. Attempting to show how well she controlled the class (class control is the most important skill for young teachers, I am told), she accused Becky of being disruptive. But she did not stop there.

"Do you even know who Shakespeare was? Do you understand his important contribution? Have you even read the assignment?"

Becky interrupted and began reciting from memory the passage that they were studying, pausing at key points to offer commentary on meaning and language use.

"It was an outstanding lecture," admitted the older English teacher, "but the timing wasn't good."

We later learned that a previous incident had cost the young student teacher her confidence, and the discipline directed toward Becky was an ill-founded attempt to recover control and dignity. In this case, both student and teacher lost.

Not all of Becky's experiences with school were this amusing; many were tragic. A lost assignment, a failed test, a skipped class, a prolonged illness, and refusals to attend school led us to see that Becky's demons were dark. We sought professional help and got a quick diagnosis of depression. Talk therapy and medication did not seem to really make things better. New doctors led to new medication and the same old results. She was up then down, but never up long enough to succeed in school. She had a job and friends, but she was clearly struggling.

The school system was not supportive. During her sophomore year, Becky figured out that she could try out for track. The physical activity would help her combat the depression, she reasoned. She thought her experience as a dancer would help her in the hurdles. Just three weeks into the season, and after only a handful of practices, Becky ran in her first and only track meet. I remember watching her with the deepest pride as she crossed the finish line in the hundred-meter hurdles forty feet behind the pack. A last-second surge was the only thing that kept her from finishing last. The next week the coach told her that her grades were not good enough to be on the team.

Becky bounced through high school like this, unable to connect with structure and finish anything. In her senior year, she enrolled in an open enrollment university. To save her the embarrassment of not graduating high school with her friends and to launch her into college, we sent her to London on a study abroad.

When she returned, the patterns of almost success continued. Her London professors described her work as "brilliant" and "graduate school level," but she did not complete her papers, and in the end, she failed one class and got a C in another. Thinking independence and a taste of the real world might wake her up, we helped her find an apartment and hoped she would find a job, but each month she came to us asking for rent to cover expenses. Our trips to various doctors continued but often ended in frustration. On one occasion, we arrived at the psychiatrist's office only to find it closed. Later we found that he had been arrested for taking his patients' Ritalin.

Throughout the ups and down of Becky's difficulties, she continued to keep a close relationship with me and her mother and talked openly about her mental illness. She was also proactive in trying to solve the problem. She tried whatever medications the therapists threw her way. She tried meditation and natural approaches. She got a therapy dog and took care of her, and it took care of her. She sought spiritual guidance from religious leaders, even though the same often criticized her.

I believe her relationship with me and her mother, her God, and her own proactive spirit saved her. At the end of her freshman year, she had been living on her own for six months. She had not found a job; she had borrowed our car but rarely went to class. Her roommates described her as sleeping most of the time. In April of that year, she came home one afternoon and asked to talk to us.

"Dad, my life is a mess. I've done nothing but dig a hole with my schooling. I can't find a job. I'm tired all the time … I don't have anything to live for. I need help … I need to stand on my own." There were no tears, just a realistic, bleak description of where she was in her miserable life.

We sat in our living room with nowhere to go, no solutions. For seven years we had tried. We had tried all combinations of depression drugs. We had tried all doctors. We had tried everything.

In my religious tradition, on rare occasions when divine guidance is needed, a father can offer a special prayer. We prayed, eyes filled with fear and tears, even anger. And then I uttered the words that I will never forget.

"Becky, this will be the best year of your life. I promise."

I will never forget the look she had on her face. It was a combination of surprise, anger, and hope—surprise that I would say such a bold thing, anger that I might be wrong, and hope that I might be right. That day we decided to start over. We decided to find a new doctor and check to see if there were physical issues aggravating the depression. Since we had begun to see our family doctor as part of the problem, we went to a doctor recommended to my wife and made an appointment.

A few days later mother, father, and daughter entered the office of Dr. Darrell Stacey, a family practitioner who, we later found out, worked a lot with patients suffering from mental illness. After a complete exam, we went in together for the consultation. It began with a familiar set of questions.

"Have you tried this drug?"

"Yes."

"Did it help?"

"No."

"Did you try it in combination with that drug?"

"Yes."

"Did it help?"

"No."

"This one?"

"Yes."

"Help?"

"No."

Finally, he came upon a drug combination she had not tried. "Can you try this for three weeks and see if it helps?"

"No," she answered.

"Why not?"

"Doctor, I haven't got three weeks."

Silence. The doctor, my wife, and I were transfixed with the honesty.

"They all say come back in three weeks, and it's not better. I just can't wait another three weeks. I don't have the fight in me anymore."

Then Dr. Stacey said words that I had been waiting to hear for seven years, words that made him an instant family hero, words that changed our lives.

"Can you come back tomorrow?" he asked.

"Yes," she agreed.

"I will see you every day you need me. I will be there with you and for you. We will beat this together, Becky. We can do this together."

Becky did not go back the next day, but she did go back the next week for blood tests and to talk. Later she tried the recommended drug combination and got a bad result. After about six weeks, Dr. Stacy called her with news.

"Becky, you have been treating depression for seven years, but you are bipolar, and many of the drug combinations we have been using on you made it worse, not better. In addition, you are hypoglycemic, which means that an empty stomach will have a devastating impact on your moods."

That was five years ago. The worst year of Becky's life became her best, with better ones since. She found a wonderful job, reentered school, and fell in love and got married. Today her wonderful husband understands her illness and is her partner in helping her stay healthy. They are now the parents of three children. Not long ago she said, "Dad, I now know what it is like to be happy."

It takes about eight hundred hours of training to get a search dog field ready; 98 percent will never have a find. But 2 percent will. That is why we still search.

PART III: HOPE

Chapter 11:

No One Is Saved without Hope

T he line between the ordinary and the extraordinary is thin, hardly visible in real time and often only seen in retrospect. As we are often disappointed when extraordinary people do ordinary things, we usually fail to notice when ordinary people do extraordinary things.

If you ask Melissa McLane, she would say she is an ordinary person. She grew up in a blue-collar Pittsburgh family with a loyal brother, a hard-working mother, and a father who encouraged her to play sports. With mostly boys in her neighborhood to play with, she learned at an early age to be street tough. Rather than play in isolation, she went out into the street with the boys, playing basketball, baseball, and whatever else the neighborhood activities menu offered. Her street-tempered sports skills led her to play in high school and college. From high school, she earned a scholarship at St. Vincent's, went on to become a leading scorer on the basketball team, and was later inducted into their sports Hall of Fame.

In all the competition, first with boys, and later with women, Melissa retained the best characteristics of her gender. Beautiful, feminine, compassionate, and nurturing, she wanted a career that would allow her to serve people. She was also competitive, tough, and resilient. Combined, these characteristics pointed her to medical school and building a practice in sports medicine. When I first met Dr. McLane, she was helping me rehabilitate a worn knee and later a broken wrist, both injuries earned while training my dog. As regular visits led to friendship, I learned she had been twice lost—once in the wilderness and once in life.

Twice Lost

The first time Melissa McLane got lost in the woods was in anticipation of fun. While in a medical residency at Alleghany Regional Hospital in Pittsburg, she joined four other professional women for a Sunday afternoon hike. The five women all worked in the hospital emergency room dealing with the full-court press of trauma every day. They were all accomplished professionals, used to working in a very stressful work environment.

The five women went to the woods north of Pittsburg, to a trail known by one of the five, and planned to hike a seven-mile loop that would take them back to their cars. It was a way to escape the demands of work, and it was also a way to talk openly about work, family, and boyfriends. The hike would also immerse them in the cleansing environment of nature under the protective canopy of a dense forest.

Because it was a marked trail and easy to see and because one of the five had done the hike before, they didn't take a map or a compass. Besides, they thought, surely the trail would be marked, and they would run into other hikers. Someone joked about running into a trauma incident, and another joked about pretending not to be doctors. The chitter-chatter of office gossip and girl talk pushed the fit and fast hikers up the trail and deeper into the thick woods full of dense, green undergrowth.

Three miles into the woods the trail began to fade. Another half mile, and it was clear that the trail was missing altogether. But heads down, they pressed on until it was difficult to see where they had come from and where they should be going. Then the light started to dim under the thick leaf canopy. Even the most highly trained emergency medical workers experience being lost with the anxiety of isolation, separation, deviation, deprivation, and realization. The realization caused one of the women to "freak out." Others turned right to where they thought the road would be. It was Melissa who focused everyone on a rational solution, defused the freak out, and developed an exit strategy.

Wearing short pants and T-shirts, they had only water bottles and snacks—no survival gear. Knowing that it was unlikely that anyone would be alerted to help search for at least twenty-four hours, the group decided to try to hike out on their own. They thrashed through the undergrowth, cutting their exposed legs on the underbrush. Before long, they found a stream, and in the dark, they followed the stream back to the road.

At the time, this was a full-grown, emotionally charged, minor injury, major stress lost incident, but because it only resulted in a twisted ankle, minor scratches, and tired bones, it just became a story told on slow days at work. Over time, it seemed to fade in significance. After all, it was just a little thing compared to the trauma that these women dealt with every day in one of America's busiest emergency rooms. But Melissa learned a life lesson not to be forgotten. When you don't know where you are, then you don't know which way to go. But when fear replaces hope, you are lost. For a moment, for one of her colleagues, fear replaced hope. That was ugly.

The second time Melissa was lost was different. It came a few years later on New Year's Eve when she was just thirty-three years old. It was the day before she planned to leave Pittsburgh for Provo, Utah. It came the day before she would start a new life as a team physician at two different universities—the day before her health insurance as a professional would kick in. On the eve of her seven-year effort to become a doctor, her parents brought her the news behind no mask of deception, no "everything will be okay."

"You have non-Hodgkin's lymphoma."

This time, there was no gradual moving through the stages of being lost. There was no slow movement through separation, to deviation, to realization. As a trained medical professional, she knew instantly that she was unforgivably lost.

"The news poured over me like scalding water. 'What?!' I said. 'What?!' Malignant? I was so stunned. The timing was so bad. My mother could not say the word *cancer*. My father was crying. My friend was the only person who could speak. After the news settled in, I began a pity party. Poor me! Then came the questions: 'Why me? What would I do? I haven't done anything yet.'" she told me.

Then she remembered being lost and what happened when one goes without hope. She began telling herself that she could make it through this. It would not be an easy road, but she could survive this. "When you take someone's hope away, they die," she said.

The change in thinking brought a new way of seeing. She said, "Then I saw the circle around me—friends and family who had always been there for me. My mother, brother, and father had never missed a game. My father went to church every day and prayed, people in my neighborhood, friends, and others rescued me with small gestures of kindness. So by the time I began treatment one month later, I really was not considering that I might die. I would never let myself think that. Never."

Where Did I Go?

In early February, Melissa began treatments. First chemotherapy and then radiation attacked the lymphoma that had attacked her body. "It was bad enough when I lost my hair. Hair is so much a part of what a woman is. Even though my mother bought me a wig, I couldn't wear it. I wore hats in public. More than once, someone called me 'sir,' and I got in their face and said, 'I am not a sir! What about "me" makes you think I am a sir?'"

She persisted through the weeks and the months, delaying the start of her medical practice and her new role as a team physician. "Cancer treatment robs you of your hair, your modesty, and your identity," she said. "One day I just looked at myself in the mirror and said, 'Where did I go?' I did not recognize the person I was looking at. Around that same time a good friend came to visit. She looked at me and asked me to take my hat off. Then she just laughed—laughed uncontrollably. I had to laugh too. It was just what I needed, such a gift."

The fight to get her body back began with a long walk around a circle of homes in her neighborhood. "I figured if I could just get around that circle every day, eventually I could get my body back." Each step in the daily walks and the weekly treatments moved her closer to becoming the doctor and not the patient. "I did not need cancer to be a good doctor. I did not need that experience to be compassionate toward my patients. I would get so mad at people who would say, 'This will make you such a good doctor.' I was already a good doctor."

It took what seemed a lifetime, or a separate life, but eventually Melissa and her family and friends celebrated the end of treatments and the return to ordinary life. But this is when this story became extraordinary.

Building the Network of Hope

Hope is an essential and renewable resource that is generated through positive interaction with others. We cannot survive without it. Hope is the fuel generated by our interactions with others that compels us to stay on the path and not get lost, to return to the path when we are lost, or to create a new path. Hope is the motivation to survive.

So when there is no hope, there is no being found. Hope is what keeps us from passing the points of separation and deviation, united with place and community. More than once, our search group has been called out to find a victim who has been lost before. The rookie searcher says, "You'd think they would learn." But they had learned. When living without hope, it is difficult to know when you have moved away from that positive social interaction that says to your heart, "Better times are ahead with loved ones around."

When we are lost and without hope, sometimes just one step in the right direction is all that it takes to begin recovery—one step, one kindness, one simple action. I have said that hope is generated by positive social interaction. It is very difficult to generate it on our own. Still, in the famous book *Between a Rock and a Hard Place*, written by Aaron Ralston, who tells his story about being trapped near Moab, Utah, he describes visioning his unborn son to create hope and motivation to escape. Trapped with his arm wedged beneath a rock, he literally cut it off with a penknife and walked out.

For most of us, hope is generated in less dramatic but equally important ways when unexpected kindness bubbles over and cleanses our wounded souls.

The Best Searchers Have Been Lost

People who can live, who can come home, who can be happy sometimes choose to continue to be lost. Others, who are facing even death, have the strength to find their way home against all odds. Choosing to live does not mean you will, but choosing to not live almost certainly means you will not. Often those who choose to live, who choose to fight, once found, want to channel their fight to helping others. The best searchers have been lost.

My friend Lois found hope in a doctor's office on the worst day of her life. After a long string of medical problems, she learned she had breast cancer. When the news came, she was in another doctor's office receiving treatment for her knee. It was Dr. Melissa McLane. The results of the mammogram, the jargon, the urgency, and the hurry-up and wait were more than she could face. Questions began to race through her mind: *What does this mean? Where do I go now? How urgent? How bad? How much pain? Can I...? Will I...? Who will care for me?*

Lois told me that Dr. McLane instantly recognized her hopelessness. Instead of becoming distant and clinical, something we are all familiar with in medical practitioners, Dr. McLane did something quite different. Lois said, "She put her arms around me, and we cried together. Then she cancelled appointments, and she went with me to the hospital to get the test results. She stayed with me until my family came.... She held my hand." Lois cannot tell this story without tears of deep, deep appreciation. "I'm so glad she was there for me on the worst day of my life."

Dr. McLane's own "worst day of her life" was why she was able to so kindly lead Lois through the wilderness of her darkest day. While it was clear that she was an exceptional and compassionate caregiver before, her own survival and victory over cancer made her the perfect rescue worker. "I hate it when people say your cancer makes you a better doctor," she told me. "I already had compassion." Still, any lost experience—one that requires us to think differently, to rely on our social networks, to purge fear in order to see clearly—changes us. We are not the same. "There were times when hope was all I had," Melissa said. But it was more than the feeling of hope—it was hope as an action verb.

The Network of Hope

Hope can be like a highly contagious disease that infects others through contact. The kindness that Melissa McLane offered is usually not the first act in a chain that can be traced through a series of special relationships. We all know that abuse is often passed on from victimizer to victim. As victims become empowered later in life, they often only know the role of victimizer and often become abusers themselves. So positive psychology tells us that the same logic must be true for healers. Just as networks of abuse can be charted and exposed, so can networks of kindness, compassion, and hope.

In my work in business and academic organizations, I have encountered many abusive managers who motivate by fear, threats, and retaliation. In interviews, they assume without question that fear is the only human motivation that leads to action. But fear is not sustainable. If the abuser—the political tyrant, the police—goes away, so does the fear. Only hope is self-sustaining. Hope does not require an oppressor, just a friend, a social network, and a kind act well received.

One year after Lois received her bad news, she reported that her year of radiation and chemotherapy had resulted in a clean mammogram. One day Lois called me up and insisted on having me give her the name and contact information of one of my colleagues whose wife had been diagnosed with breast cancer just the day before. I did not know my colleague's wife, and neither did Lois, so I was reluctant. But Lois was more insistent than I was reluctant, and she succeeded in extracting from me the contact information. She called without reservation and offered to help. A four-hour conversation ensued. Today these two women who were once strangers are working together to beat this disease together.

Now I Am Found

Being found by a fellow cancer survivor who understands perfectly what you are going through, or a fellow alcoholic who has managed to become sober, or just a fellow traveler who cares, often does not prevent the suffering that recovery demands. But it does create an essential element—hope.

It may seem like a random coincidence when you are in the right place at the right time with the right person—luck—but Dr. McLane and many others see it differently. "There is no way in all my doctor's rational mind that I believe that meeting Melissa was a coincidence," Lois said. "Someone is looking out for her … and me."

In the Christian text of the New Testament, Jesus tells the now-famous story of the prodigal son who left his father and brother and took his inheritance and wasted it. He came to himself. Every lost person who is found comes to himself. He realizes he is lost, and then he begins to take the steps to be found and to come home. The prodigal son returned to his family, offering to be but a servant, but his father called out in praise saying, "He was lost and now he is found." (Luke 15:32)

This parable only hints at some of the trouble to come in this family, for once someone is lost, he is never the same. I am sure that the father, the mother, the once-lost son, and the always-loyal brother had much to work out. I am sure that the once-lost son lives through other times when separation and deviation seemed like the better course. Reunification is not easy, but hope is the tie that binds.

Psychology has long recognized the power of hope and the pit of hopelessness. Traditional psychology has given us the term "learned helplessness." Psychologist Martin Seligman showed first with dogs and then with humans that negative conditions can produce a passive reaction. That is, the dogs and the people just rolled over and let bad things happen without trying to make their own situations better. This certainly describes David. In later studies, it was learned that subject who has a pessimistic explanatory style (think Eeyore from the Winnie the Pooh stories) were more likely to have feelings of depression and helplessness. In these cases, subjects felt like it was their fault, things would never change, and help would not help. This also described David. Seligman believes that cognitive therapy can help people identify their negative scripts and replace them with positive scripts, this helping with the effects of learned helplessness.

After identifying psychological disorders and treating psychologically sick patients for years, Seligman had a simple and profound realization that turned the field of psychology. He realized that if he could take sick people and make them well, why not take well people and make them stronger? In other words, if people could learn hopelessness, why could they not learn hopefulness?

This realization caught fire in the field of psychology and led to the development of a field call "positive psychology." In 1990, Seligman published a book called *Learned Optimism*. In that book, he documents how optimists are higher achievers and have better health and better relationships. He says optimistic people believe bad events are temporary. Throughout this book, we see how people who are lost in the wilderness, work, or life see their situations as something that will pass. They will be reunited. They will find meaningful work. They will be healed. The belief does help create the reality—not always, but often.

Optimistic people also compartmentalize their helplessness. The "freak out moments" (remember the Boy Scout named Jared) do not happen or are quickly reigned in. The bad things that happened in one part of your life don't poison all your life. This is Dr. Melissa McLane. As she faced her own challenges, as she battled her cancer, she continued to treat others with compassion and kindness. Her own problem was contained and did not pillage and poison the rest of what is good in her life. Like Melissa, people who are lost in the wilderness, work, and life shine the bright light of hope that happens in one part of their lives on all parts of their lives.

In addition, optimists blame bad events on causes outside themselves. They see good things as something caused by them, and bad things as having external causes. They see negative events as temporary conditions and positive events as permanent. Melissa McLane told me that she had a brief pity party for a day or so and then took on the cancer. She lost her hair through chemotherapy. She lost weight. She lost physical strength but not inner strength.

"When I was recovering in my parents' home in Pittsburgh," she told me, "I would try to walk around this circle of homes. Every day I would go out and try to get around the circle. I knew that if I could get around those homes every day, if I could just make it around, I could live." Each day, each step, each time around the circle took her closer to healing.

Throughout this book, we have heard the stories of those who sat on the boundary of hopelessness and hopefulness, of being lost and being found. They made a choice to go one way or another. Some, like David, stayed lost. They struggled and finally chose hopelessness. Others, like Albert Chretien, wanted to be found but were overwhelmed by circumstances. The lessons of the lost come from people like Lois, Melissa, Sue and Ray, Jared, and Rita who chose hopefulness. It was their first step toward being found, toward coming home. Earlier in this book, I described the story of Amy Racina who, while on a solo hike in the Sierra Nevada Mountains, took a serious fall. After several days in agony, she was rescued. During the time she was lying on the ground not knowing if anyone would find her, she came to herself. She realized what she wanted for that moment and always was to be hopeful.

"Sometimes I have experienced ambivalence. Is life a good thing? Is it worth going on? Now, faced with the ultimate question, 'How much do you want to live,' I find I do, very much, want to live. There is no doubt whatsoever. Despite my understanding that there are no guarantees, I am determined to do whatever I can to make life the probable outcome. I want to live. That sweet moment of total assurance becomes a treasure in my memory, because for one glowing second, I experienced absolutely no ambivalence. I want to live. My decision is made." (Racina, 2005)

In the second chapter of this book, I wrote about Victoria Grover who survived in the Escalante Desert for four days, three of those days with a broken leg. After thinking about it for a long time, Victoria admitted that she had entered the wilderness already lost. "I came out to Utah feeling really exhausted," she said. "I had felt for the last few months that I was lost to myself. Others would not see it, but I was out of step with my normal me. When I got on that trail, I was flying, leaving my troubles behind. I made a mistake going further and deeper into the wilderness because it took me further away from my troubles."

She ran out of water. She had no more fuel to build a warning fire. She had limited shelter. She slipped into hallucinations and hypothermia. But she did not lose hope. There is no pathway home without first feeling and seeing hope.

For Victoria, faith is an action verb. Faith is what you do to show that you believe that a better situation is possible. "Faith," she said, "is my part in the success equation."

What is hope then? It is the sweet time between actions when we wait, we think, and we believe that good things are next. To be sure, hope is not always accurate. Victoria hoped that searchers were looking for her on the first day. They did not start searching until the third day. Melissa McLane hoped that beating cancer meant a healthy life, but while she is cancer free, the cancer treatment has left her with other unanticipated health challenges. Most of us hope for something that does not fully materialize. But hope involved not just seeing success but accepting the good in any circumstance.

Almost everyone I interviewed for this book who survived being lost or who survived the loss of a loved one said some version of the same thing: "I would not wish this difficulty one anyone, not even my worst enemy. I would never have willingly gone onto this wilderness on my own. But now that I am through it, I am a new person—a different person—and I would not trade that for anything."

Cancer, bereavement, addiction, a career crisis, the breakup of a family, leaving home, coming home, or being lost in the wilderness—we would never wish those on others, but they are also the life-tempering experiences that allow us to move higher, farther, and deeper into this world.

After being lost, why do searchers search in a different way, doctors practice medicine in a different way, teachers teach in a different way, leaders lead in a different way, parents parent in a different way, and people live life in a different way? Because they have been lost. We all have. And when we are found, we can be forever changed by hope.

Chapter 12:

Forever Changed

At my ten-year high school reunion, we each wrote a paragraph for the program about our lives. Most of the eight hundred members of the graduating class responded. We came from country club privilege, fine families with education and career opportunities. Most of us were continuing the legacy of privilege untouched by the brush of fate. We did our best to make the most of what we had, so after ten years, we had careers and families to brag about. We had traveled internationally and published books. There were college degrees and graduate schools, law firm partnerships, medical school residencies, and successful businesses. It was the chest beating of a young generation who seemed invulnerable in an otherwise harsh world, and I beat my chest right alongside my colleagues. I had a high-profile job as a news reporter on local television. I had a beautiful wife. I had children. I had an untarnished life.

But there were also signs that all was not right. We were just ten years out of high school, and seven of the eight hundred had died early deaths—two from AIDS, three suicides. My debate partner and friend, Steve Halgren, had been killed by a drunk driver coming home from work. So had the girl who lived down the street, Jan Nielson. Others had dropped off the map, disappeared, unwilling to participate in the subtle competition called a high school reunion. The random rotation of the universe had taken its toll. There was a crack in the confidence, a rift in the ignorance that protected us.

At the twenty-year reunion, there were still the brags of careers, kids, even grandkids, and accomplishments. But there were also honest stories of divorce, illness overcome, illness not to be overcome, the death of a child, or the death of a spouse. There were the deaths of classmates too—overdose, cancer, a bike accident, a car wreck and brain injury, an arrest, a sentence.

More were lost. Some were just surviving. But many were willing to say that they were coming home from a long absence.

"I was an alcoholic. Been one since high school"

"I was fired from my job, and I have been struggling ever since."

"Our family business went belly up when I took over the management."

"I lost my faith."

"I lost my loved one."

"I never found someone to marry."

Some of the stories of the untouched had turned to stories of redemption, rebuilding, and reunification: "I divorced and then later married my one love from high school—my true love." Like a flashback to junior prom, several had rediscovered high school romance and made it stick this time.

Now at thirty years, some are jaded and cynical. Some are not willing to tell their stories. They want to remain anonymous and free of judgment. But then there are those who are more realistic, respectful, and hopeful. The casualties have mounted, but most of us have wandered and come home to a more peaceful and profound existence. We have been lost and found in our careers, our lives, and in our own self-made wilderness. We are better for it. We realize being lost is a natural condition. We respect, even admire, those who can make it home, and we are hopeful that the loved ones we search for will be with us again.

I have spent long days searching in below-freezing temperatures and oppressive heat, in wilderness and urban environments. For days, I've walked many miles, watching my dog, hoping that his nose will point up to catch a scent and then he will turn and follow that scent to its source. There have been times when he has "alerted," turned into the wind, and led me, sometimes for miles, up a canyon or across wide meadow to find someone who was not lost or to another searcher. We have never been the first ones to find a victim. As I said earlier, most search dogs never have a find.

Still, in those long and grueling days when dog and handler come back exhausted and unaccomplished, when the search yields nothing, I have found myself. I have found who I want to be and what I want to do. I have found my voice in writing—not the academic voice, but the real and personal voice—and so has my voiceless companion named Dusty. He loves his work. He yearns for the long day, the big search, and hopefully, someday, the find. Our new sense of purpose has also helped me see other lost people who are all around me, not just in the wilderness, but also in my work and in my community.

Lost in the Bookstore

In a local bookstore café, men are eyeing me as I write this final chapter, not in a threatening way, but asking if I'm part of the brotherhood. The look and nod and whisper, "Is he a new member of the club?" Perhaps I am someone who found this coffee and books place the same way they did, because they have lots of time and a burning need. But I do not have lots of time or the same burning need. I have a purpose, a place to go, an identity. I have a job.

From ten o'clock in the morning to two o'clock in the afternoon every weekday, the bookstore café is the new soup line, but with no soup. It has become a gathering place for middle-aged men hoping to reinvent themselves into economic relevance. There is free access to the web and books and magazines full of career advice that can be read but don't need to be bought. They come because they want a place to go and someone to talk to. They are white, forty-plus men, middle class. They were once educated. Most have college degrees that have worn out for lack of use. They once aspired to leadership or management, but their careers did not turn out the way they hoped, and they were forced to settle for middle management or individual contributor jobs that pay less than they had hoped. Some have been divorced, but those who have not can see it coming, as they can no longer provide the financial and emotional security that is their contribution to a marriage relationship.

In the middle row of the twenty tables sits the English teacher. He is slight in figure, with a 1960s beard, wire-rim glasses, and an army surplus pack for a briefcase. He abandoned the corporate look eighteen months ago on the worst day of his life when he was fired from a job he really did not want. He gave up a beloved job teaching high school English five years ago to take a job in a corporate technical writing center. He had hated that job, but the salary was good and he could finally pay the bills. But a year and a half ago the outsourcing angel of death visited his company, and his job was sent to India. He was the first to start coming to the café, and he has seen many come and go.

"He helps us with our resumes and letters," says one man. "No charge." Even if he wanted to charge, no one could afford to pay him.

These men are above temporary work, though every once in a while someone will disappear for a week and return. He'll come into the café and buy something to drink. For the first time in months, he has a few dollars to spend. For the first time in months, he has half an ounce of self-respect, not fabricated, but created when a man adds value to his family through work, even if it is temporary.

One member of the group took a retail sales job during Christmas. A big mistake, he said. "One of my neighbors bought something from me and said 'I didn't know you had sunk so low.' Other people I knew would just pretend to not see me or, if they did talk, would say things like, 'Oh, my daughter who is in high school works here.'"

You can tell the newcomers. You can tell the freshly unemployed. They come into the café with stacks of books on job search topics—how to write a résumé, how to write a killer letter, how to interview. They don't want to buy the books, but they do want the latest ideas. So they read and explore, taking notes on hand-me-down laptops that make them miss the technology they handed in when they lost their jobs. "I'm even using the cell phone that we replaced last year because my daughter wanted an upgrade," said one man.

They have a disease. The disease is fear—fear of being irrelevant. It is not contagious, but people treat you as if it is. They think coming in contact with your fear will force them to see how easy it would be for them to be there, with you, in the café, looking. So they treat you with rubber gloves and enter into quick, I'm-in-a-hurry conversations. They don't want to linger. Soon the only people who really listen are other unemployed men—the brotherhood of the book café.

When a newcomer comes to the café, someone will approach him and start a conversation. "Looking for work?"—a question from a stranger. Starved for friendly and real conversation, he'll tell his story. It's the same story, the same plot. The company is different. The people involved are different. But the story is the same.

"Those younger bosses don't understand the value I bring to the company."

"I should have gone for my MBA."

"They handled the terminations in a callous, uncaring way."

"They would not have fired me if I were a woman or minority."

"None of my colleagues, the people I worked with for years, will return my calls."

"My severance is running out, and I thought I would have something by now."

"My family and friends don't know how to help, so they stop trying."

The regulars start their sessions by opening up their laptops and looking at the latest listings. They hit all the websites now familiar, so they can say they are trying. When they first started looking, they fired off their resumes right and left, shooting at anything that moved. But that costs too much, not economically but emotionally. They were forced to become more selective, because the cost of the disappointment of not getting the job or not getting the interview or not even getting a call renewed the hurt of getting fired. So they budget their disappointment.

Now they only go after the jobs they really want. They find a corner and craft their letters and résumés, even role-playing interviews, saying all along that they don't really want the job that they would give almost anything to have. The English teacher reads their letters. He makes changes carefully, so as not to hurt a fragile man who never expected to be in a job search. Quietly and proudly, he claims he helped three men write letters that led to jobs. They finally escaped the café for better places. But then again, almost anyplace is a better place.

For most, when the phone does not ring, when the résumé fails to impress or open doors, they settle into a routine. They come every day. They sit at a table. They scan the net, download a job opportunity, and check e-mail. Someone, just one person, joins them. They never sit in a large group, rarely more than pairs. Then they talk, commiserate, complain. They share the pain and then try to listen. By midafternoon, they collect their belongings. The lucky ones have to pick up the kids, because the wife is working. The others go home to television, chores, and dinner. Fitness clubs and restaurants are no longer in the budget. They have already had the best part of their day.

Across the parking lot in view of the café a "homeless" man works a sign. His appeal prop, made to look desperate on tattered cardboard, promises a willingness to work. On cold days, he does better, they observe with resentment.

"He knows what he is doing, and he's never going to work," says one man over his résumé. "He has a scam, a racket. I've got my pride."

"Watch—he makes more than I did when I was working," says another, loud enough for everyone to hear.

If you sit there long enough, you will hear a long pause, then the words of deep pain spoken in a fearless monotone that is now at the foundation of their being. They are lost in an unfamiliar land. Their identity went out with the job. They are irrelevant in society, in their own families, in their marriages. They have become burdens. So they deal with their pain with evermore grandiose stories about their own importance, about their own misunderstood significance—stories of injustice, of victimhood, of unrecognized value.

For many, the disappointment extends to their parents. Their own fathers and mothers have retired, career and reputation fixed. Their place in history is etched in a small but legible stone: "We did something with our lives." They lived through a war and recessions, through personal and family crises, and kept their financial footing. But their boy can't hold a job, can't manage a career. Sometimes the humiliation of unemployment is compounded when the boy, the man, moves in with elderly parents in a giant step backward.

All the time, the questions follow, swirling around them like a tornado. It's too late to get an MBA, or is it? How could we afford it anyway with the kids needing college? Would it really help? Should I take a lesser job that destroys my résumé? Makes me look desperate? Then, when they apply to the lesser jobs, they don't get them. They are overqualified. They don't value my experience. They hired a blank slate, not someone with experience. They hired younger.

Over time, these broken men do not understand that the cynical toxic attitude that is verbalized in this safe place cannot be shed in a job interview, or even in a conversation with a friend or family member. It has a stench that repels all opportunity, large and small. They cannot wash it off or cover it with the perfume of professionalism. It is their disease.

Frustrated that the men were occupying half of the tables in the café and not buying coffee or three-dollar bottles of Italian water, the bookstore manager tried to run them out. First he tried subtly, by cutting power to the outlets where the computers were charging. But then the men came with laptops fully charged. Next, the café manager would bring around menus and hollowly ask if they were ready to order every twenty minutes. Sorry, no jobs on the menus. Then, finally, he posted time limit signs: "Please be courteous to other customers and limit ..."—ignored.

But the bookstore did hire the English teacher at the help desk. He's making less than he did in the corporation, less even than he did as a schoolteacher, but hey, it's a job.

Lost at School

I retreat to my office at the university—no wandering eyes here. But there is a steady stream of students with questions. It is hard to write with these interruptions. Early in my career I was told by a department chair to ration my time with students, keep to office hours. Don't let them invade your space for writing and research. Then I saw the statistics. Half the freshmen who enter an American university, who have the opportunity coveted by most of the world, do not return for their sophomore years. They get lost.

The reasons are many. They lack money or motivation. They have relationship problems, substance abuse, depression, or a combination of these. Some find their own way back. Most can be rescued with a caring conversation and careful direction. They need a parent, a mentor, or a professor. It cost me tenure at my first university, but my policy for students is simple: you can call me any time for any reason. Any they do. But rather than keep me from research and writing and personal development, the things I am supposed to be doing as a professor, it has focused me on what I should be doing as an educator. The payoff has been inspiring, as I hear and see in real time people overcoming the next generation of difficulties to find themselves in a better place.

I pity my colleagues who see their careers in education as a place of intellectual self-indulgence. They see their gifts and talents, which exceed mine, as a reason to become isolated from the very society that has offered them a privileged place. These people are also lost. They have jobs, they come to work, and they have regular contact with sometimes admiring students. But they have lost touch with the *why* of education. They have forgotten that they too were once ignorant and unread. They have become habitually isolated from the very social order that feeds them and gives them relevance.

Previously in this book I have cited Wendell Berry, who said, "If you don't know where you are from, you don't know who you are." (Berry, 1972) In this simple yet profound statement, he surfaces a truth about our human geography. Said in different terms, if you do not know who you are, if you do not know who you want to be with, if you do not know where you want to be, if home has no meaning for you, then it is hard to feel lost. So many people who are the subject of searches—in work, life, or the wilderness—fall into this category. They do not want to be found, or they do not know that they are lost. In not recognizing that they are lost, they rob themselves of the very learning experience that would give their life meaning.

It is an ironic blessing that being lost and found is a deep reminder of the value of home. In the first chapter, I described Victoria Grover's survival experience in the southern Utah Desert. Several times in the interviews she referred to her "cherished experience." She also admitted that she had some of the symptoms of post-traumatic stress disorder. PTSD has a clinical definition, but it is simply when a lost person found takes with them the trauma of the experience. While our physical beings might be restored to our homes, the wilderness lingers in our minds. The fear still grips the mind, and our shame persists. Shame is a hard thing to discard.

Still, the learning that we gain from being lost outweighs the sometimes-persistent fear that follows us home. Victoria called it the "cherished experience." It was certainly life changing. A few months after returning home, Victoria wrote, "I've been working my way through the 'acute stress' recovery this past week, the unfocused anxiety and all the other emotions, so unfamiliar to me, of being disconnected from everything. I am much better today than I was a week ago. Being stuck in that one place for those days was awful but at the time I kept thinking of the things I could do, I had to do, to stay alive—arranging and rearranging my poncho around me to keep wind out and warmth in, doing exercises with my arms, making noise in threes like banging rocks together or yelling three shouts—keeping my skin covered so I wouldn't get sunburned—somehow that protected me from feeling too helpless."

When she was rescued, and when she gifted me her story for this book, her ordeal was not over. There was still a lingering fear and helplessness. Remember, being lost is not just about being in the wrong place. It is not just about being physically deviated, separated, isolated, and deprived. It is about realizing our constant vulnerabilities. Those feelings often linger, but we learn to live with them. Victoria said, "Right after I came *home* and was finally safe and had others to take care of me, *then* the feeling of being so stuck became fuel for the fear and helplessness and the incredible disconnection I felt the first day or two back. But I'm getting through that, I guess the same way I got through the days in the desert—talking to myself, reading encouraging things about recovering from fear, and beginning to find the places where this new knowledge is going to strengthen and enlarge my life, make me a better, stronger, more compassionate human. Good people here are helping me too, just supporting and encouraging me, accepting me."

Like so many people who are lost and then found, Victoria has accelerated her own recovery by serving others. She threw herself back into her medical practice, her community and church service, and her family. But she also sees the world around her with a wider-angle lens. And she sees with greater compassion the plight of lost people everywhere. Again, with full generosity of heart, Victoria said, "Tell anybody anything you want to from my story that you think would help them. "

Her words bring up the delicate and difficult question of how to help those who are lost. What do we do? What can we say? Where can we search? How much can we give? What if they don't know they are lost? What if they don't want to be found?

We all encounter lost people every day. They may not have yet reached the points of separation, isolation, deviation, deprivation, and realization described earlier in this book. If they have not, then there is time to help them reconnect, restore, and recommit. Preventive measures are always so much less costly than a search where the randomness of nature can remove the possibility of positive outcome.

The inconvenient truth of all searches—in work, life, or the wilderness—is that the search effort does not correspond to the outcome. I was a small part of a massive search for Al Chretien. Thousands of hours and Herculean efforts by an under-resourced search team over eighteen months led to nothing. Then a hunter stepped around a tree, saw a backpack in the dirt, and then found the remains up under a tree a few feet away. I have also been on a poorly organized search where communication and coordination were a problem. The search strategy was wrong, but the subjects were found despite the chaotic effort. Author David Guterson wrote, "Accident rules every corner of the universe, except the chambers of the human heart." (Guterson, 1991) His idea suggests that our intentions to find, rescue, and rehabilitate a subject are always subject to the random chaos that nature, society, and our work communities provide. Our best efforts can fall short, and our worst efforts can yield spectacular results. If you are a parent who has lost a child to mental illness, an employer who has lost a colleague to addiction, or a partner who has lost a spouse to indifference, then you know that your efforts can make all the difference or no difference.

But you try anyway.

If my experience as a searcher has taught me anything, it is that once-lost people make the best searchers. Most of my SAR colleagues have been lost in work, life, or the wilderness. They know. They might not know any better where to look, and they might not know any better how to look, but they know why to look. Once you feel the deep loneliness of being lost, you cannot turn away.

Every few weeks my pager goes off, and I find myself in a mountain or desert parking lot at an incident command center. A local sheriff has organized a search. First come the cars and SUVs with qualified search volunteers. Some are members of the local SAR team. Others have driven for hours from faraway places. These people, many who were once lost themselves and who have special skills and training, are coming and saying, "How can we help?" They strategize and deploy, lending urgency to the moment, especially if the subject was last seen alive. Then the local people come—friends and relatives—wanting to help but not wanting to get in the way. They bring food and support for the SAR teams. And they cheer when there is a live find and comfort and cry when there is not.

Lost people often return to be in that group, to be searchers of some kind. They return to find an expanded role of helping. They reduce their own sense of helplessness by helping others, creating a new cycle of good. Victoria Grover wrote me as I was completing this book and said it best. She wrote, "When I hear news of people being lost, then found, and I wonder if there's anyone who does for them what you did for me. Talks to them afterward, comforts them in their shame, and gives them ideas and a possible future to hold onto when they still feel lost even after they're found. I'm going to find out about that, because that is certainly one thing I could do."

I could do it. You could do it, anyone could do it. Someone will always search. It is part of our nature to want to reconnect the human family.

Early in 2014, Salt Lake Tribune reporter Paul Rolley included this letter in his column.

"My name is Jordan. A little over two years ago I tried to kill myself in this very park. I was only 16 and thought that my problems were so horrible that the best way to deal with them was to escape them. I was oh so very wrong

"On 11-11-11, I fell off the side of this cliff. I don't know where I was found or who found me. But to that early-morning jogger that found me on 11-12-11, thank you.

"You saved my life and I can never repay you for that. I hope you still take this path and that you somehow see this because I want you to know that I'm OK and it's because of you that I am. So thank you."

Jordan and others who have been rescued need to know that being saved also saves us. It helps us put our own live in perspective. It helps us find a purpose. It also reminds us about when we were lost and needed a hand, a heart and a life from someone else.

In December 2013, Marissa Barry of Portage, Michigan came home from school after a bad day. Marissa did what I do after a bad day. She went to the woods. For me there is something about nature that scrubs the anger and frustration from the soul and gives me perspective. Perhaps this is what she was seeking. She told reporters that she often walked in the woods, even on freezing cold days like this one.

On this day she wandered too far, into unfamiliar forest and got lost. The thick underbrush made it difficult for her to see, to gain perspective. The cold was draining her energy. She walked, stumbled and fell. Then she walked again, trying to find her way out of the maze and back to civilization.

Her family noticed her missing, and within a few hours a search was mounted. Like most hasty situations, authorities did not know if she was with friends hanging out at a local restaurant, lost in the woods, or been abducted. Within a few hours helicopters had joined the search and the news media was broadcasting her picture. Meanwhile, Marissa was becoming increasingly disoriented and more hypothermic. "My eyes were open, but I just couldn't see. It all felt like I was still dreaming," she told a reporter.

The search continued through the night and into the next day. Police were concerned that if they did not find her within 24 hours she would parish. Police are often driven by those kinds of statistics. But Marissa was just trying to put one foot in front of the other and find a way out of the woods. She had lost a glove, and somehow lost her boot. Her mind was foggy. "I remember waking up and seeing my gloves on the ground next to me, and I was wondering why they were there. I think I had shed my gloves off without consciously knowing it," said Marissa.

"Then my whole body was cold and shivering, but at the same time I felt warm because hypothermia does that to you. It makes you feel warm. So, I felt really warm at the same time, but I also felt cold. So, it felt like I was having a fever."

Shivering and unable to move forward, she did the only thing she could, the only thing that was available, she shook the tree that was holding her up. She shook it hard and tried to call out, but her voice was not working.

Several hundred feet away, along a highway, a small road crew was making repairs when they saw a moving tree in the still forest. It was puzzling. Why would a tree be moving? Animals don't do that. They knew that a young girl was missing, and so they walked into the woods to find Marissa, literally minutes from death.

Marissa's recovery has been difficult. One month after the ordeal, she was facing foot amputation due to frostbite. She told a reporter, "Life may be rough. You may not know that you have a purpose in life. But, in reality, you do have purpose in life and there's a reason why you're here and you may not know it yet. But you're still living to find out why you're here, and it may take years, but you're going to be alive for a reason. I'm here to find out."

So am I. We all are.

Bibliography

Berry, Wendell. *A Continuous Harmony: Essays Cultural and Agricultural*. New York: Harcourt, Brace, 1972.

Durkheim, Emile. *Suicide*. New York: Free Press, 1979.

Frankl, Viktor. *Man's Search for Meaning: An Introduction to Logotherapy*. Boston: Beacon Press, 2006.

Gonzales, Laurence. *Deep Survival: Who Lives, Who Dies, and Why*. New York: Norton, 2004.

Griffith, Cary. *Lost in the Wild*. St. Paul: Borealis Books, 2006.

Guterson, David. *Snow Falling on Cedar*. New York: Harcourt, Brace, 1994.

Heth, C. D., and E. H. Cornell. "A Geographic Information System for Managing Search for Lost Persons." In *Applied Spatial Cognition: From Research to Cognitive Technology*, edited by G. L. Allen. Mahwah, NJ: Lawrence Earlbaum Associates, 2007.

Hill, Kenneth. *Lost Person Behaviour.* Ottawa: National SAR Secretariat, 1998.

_____. "Spatial Competence of Elderly Hunters." *Environment and Behavior* 24 (1992): 798–813.

_____. "Wayfinding and Spatial Reorientation by Nova Scotia Deer Hunters." *Environment and Behavior.* (2011): 1–17.

International Search and Rescue Incident Database (ISRID) (2012). Accessed June 1, 2012. http://www.dbs-sar.com/ SAR_Research/ISRID.htm.

Koester, Robert. *Lost Person Behavior: A Search and Rescue Guide on Where to Look—for Land, Air, and Water.* Charlottesville, VA: dbs. Productions, 2008.

Kübler-Ross, Elizabeth. *On Death and Dying.* New York: Rutledge, 1998.

Maclean, Norman. *A River Runs Through It.* Chicago: University of Chicago Press, 1989.

Mills, Helms. *Making Sense of Organizational Change.* London: Rutledge, 1998.

Montello, D. R. "What It Means to Be Lost." *Proceedings of the Search and Rescue Secretariat of Canada (SARSCENE), Banff, Alberta, Canada.* Ottawa: National Search and Rescue Secretariat, 1998.

Oxford English Dictionary. *Oed.com.*

Palmer, Parker. *A Hidden Wholeness: The Journey Toward an Undivided Life.* San Francisco: Jossey Bass, 2004.

Racina, Amy. *Angels in the Wilderness.* Santa Rosa, CA: Elite Books, 2005.

Schlenker, B. *Impression Management: The Self-Concept, Social Identity, and Interpersonal Relations.* Monterey, CA: Brooks/Cole, 1980.

Seligman, Martin. *Learned Optimism: How to Change your Mind and Change your Life.* New York: Pocket Books, 1990.

Shapiro, Fred. *Yale Book of Quotations.* New Haven, Connecticut: Yale University Press.

Sherwood, Ben. *The Survivors Club: The Secrets and Science that Could Save Your Life.* New York: Grand Central Publishing, 2009.

Sutcliffe, K. M. "Organizational Environments and Organizational Information Processing." In *Handbook of Organizational Communication: Advances in Theory, Research, and Methods,* edited by F. Jablin and L. Putnam. Beverly Hills: Sage, 2000.

Sutcliffe, K. M. and T. J. Vogus. "Organizing for Resilience." In *Positive Organizational Scholarship,* edited by K. Cameron, J. E. Dutton, and R. E. Quinn. San Francisco: Berrett-Koehler Publishers, 2003.

Syrotuck, William. *Analysis of Lost Person Behavior.* New York: Arner Publications, 1997.

Tedeschi, J. T. and M. Riess. "Identities, the Phenomenal Self, and Laboratory Research." In *Impression Management Theory and Social Psychological Research*, edited by James T. Tedeschi. New York: Academic Press, 1984.

Tugade, M. M. and B. L. Fredrickson. "Resilient Individuals Use Positive Emotions to Bounce Back from Negative Emotional Experiences." Journal of Personality and Social Psychology 86 (2004): 320–333.

Weick, Karl. "Enacted Sensemaking in Crisis Situations." *Journal of Management Studies* 25, no. 4 (1988): 305–17.

_____. *Sensemaking in Organizations*. Thousand Oaks, CA: Sage Publications, 1994.

_____. *Making Sense of the Organization*. Vol. 1. New York: Blackwell Publishing, 2001.

_____. *Making Sense of the Organization*. Vol. 2. New York: John Wiley & Sons, 2009.

_____. *The Social Psychology of Organizing*. New York: Addison-Wesley, 1989.

Weick, Karl, and Kathleen Sutcliffe. *Managing the Expected: Resilience Performance in an Age of Uncertainty*. San Francisco: Jossey-Bass, 2007

Wolfe, Thomas. *You Can't Go Home Again*. New York: Simon and Schuster, 1934.

The Gift of the Story

Tell your lost-and-found story to others.

Telling lost stories helps reestablish relationships and cement hope. They help you and help others understand the plot and the context for life-changing events. This book would not have been possible without Victoria Grover, Lois Ritchie, Sue and Ray Baird, Melissa McLane, and others who trusted me with their stories and led me to the lessons of the lost.

Post your lost-and-found story and read the stories of others at:

http://lessonsofthelost.com

Hammond's Video Blog:

See the author's training and real search video blog at:

http://lessonsofthelost.com or on the Stillwaterfork YouTube channel

Scott Hammond is available for speeches and training for corporations, educational institutions, churches, and nonprofit organizations. Please contact him at scott@lessonsofthelost.com.

The Author

Scott C. Hammond is a volunteer search and rescue worker with Rocky Mountain Rescue Dogs. He is also a professor of management in the Jon M. Huntsman School of Business at Utah State University, teaching undergraduates and in the MBA program.

As an organizational development consultant who specializes in scenario

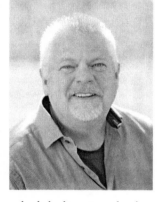

planning, strategic planning processes, and globalization, he has worked with clients such as Alticor (Amway), Monsanto, Boart Longyear, Intermountain Health Care, KSL Television (NBC), the National Parks Service, NCS Education, the Los Alamos National Laboratory, the Idaho National Engineering Laboratory, Exxon, General Dynamics, Colorado OBGYN Society, KBYU Television (PBS), General Electric, the North Monterey Unified School District, and others.

Scott holds a master's degree in organizational behavior from Brigham Young University and a PhD in communication from the University of Utah. He has published numerous articles on organizational change, leadership, and dialogic problem solving.

He is currently writing on paradigm change and ideological conflict in culturally complex organizations. This includes applying lost person behavior psychology to organizations. Hammond is a regular speaker for corporate events and education, and guest on talk radio stations nationwide.

In addition to his professional work, Scott is a volunteer search-and-rescue worker with Rocky Mountain Rescue Dogs and a member of the National Search and Rescue Association. He enjoys backpacking, camping, cross-country skiing, and visiting national parks with his wife and five children.

Dusty the Wonder Dog

Dusty is a purebred golden retriever and a Level III (RMRD Standards) search dog with specific training in area search, human remains detection, and tracking. He often attends training, speeches, and presentations with his training partner. When he is not training, he is fruitlessly pursuing his lifelong ambition to rid the world of the evil menace of ground squirrels.

Open Book Editions
A Berrett-Koehler Partner

Open Book Editions is a joint venture between Berrett-Koehler Publishers and Author Solutions, the market leader in self-publishing. There are many more aspiring authors who share Berrett-Koehler's mission than we can sustainably publish. To serve these authors, Open Book Editions offers a comprehensive self-publishing opportunity.

A Shared Mission

Open Book Editions welcomes authors who share the Berrett-Koehler mission—Creating a World That Works for All. We believe that to truly create a better world, action is needed at all levels—individual, organizational, and societal. At the individual level, our publications help people align their lives with their values and with their aspirations for a better world. At the organizational level, we promote progressive leadership and management practices, socially responsible approaches to business, and humane and effective organizations. At the societal level, we publish content that advances social and economic justice, shared prosperity, sustainability, and new solutions to national and global issues.

Open Book Editions represents a new way to further the BK mission and expand our community. We look forward to helping more authors challenge conventional thinking, introduce new ideas, and foster positive change.

For more information, see the Open Book Editions website: http://www.iuniverse.com/Packages/OpenBookEditions.aspx

Join the BK Community! See exclusive author videos, join discussion groups, find out about upcoming events, read author blogs, and much more! http://bkcommunity.com/

CPSIA information can be obtained
at www.ICGtesting.com
Printed in the USA
FSOW02n1936260416
19735FS